The Gabriel Moraga Expedition Of 1806: The Diary Of Fray Pedro Munoz: The Huntington Library Quarterly, May 1946

Pedro Munoz

THE
Huntington Library
Quarterly

A Journal for the History and

Interpretation of English and American History

MAY, 1946 ◆ VOLUME IX, NUMBER 3

HUNTINGTON LIBRARY : SAN MARINO, CALIFORNIA

The Huntington Library Quarterly is published four times a year by
Henry E. Huntington Library and Art Gallery, San Marino, California

———

Subscription Price $5.00 a Year; Single Numbers $1.50
Entered as second-class matter October 6, 1937
at the post office at Pasadena, California
under the Act of March 3, 1879

Contents

THE

HUNTINGTON LIBRARY

QUARTERLY

NUMBER 3   MAY, 1946

Dr. Edwin Francis Gay

O N FEBRUARY 7, 1946, the Huntington Library sustained a major loss in the death of Dr. Edwin F. Gay, who had served as Chairman of the Research Group since the time of Dr. Max Farrand's retirement as Director, in June, 1941. Dr. Gay's influence within the Huntington Library was exercised during the last decade of a versatile and distinguished life. The Library was fortunate in securing his presence, since Dr. Gay brought with him the accumulated wisdom of so many fruitful years, joined to a mind still keen with intellectual curiosity and ardent in the unending search for truth.

The foundations of Dr. Gay's scholarship were laid in a twelve-year period of European study, concluded by the taking of his doctorate from the University of Berlin in 1902 and by the publication of his researches in the sixteenth century enclosure movement in England. From 1902 to 1919 he taught at Harvard, becoming a full professor there in 1906. Dr. Gay was the first Dean of the Harvard Graduate School of Business Administration, from 1908 to 1919, and was largely responsible for the development of that school's reputation as the foremost in the world for professional business training. During the First World War he left the academic life to serve with the United States Shipping Board, becoming chairman of the Division of Planning and Statistics of the War Industries Board and also of the Central Bureau of Planning and Statistics. These federal appointments furthered the wartime economic mobilization of this country, in particular making available a greatly increased tonnage of shipping for military uses.

In 1920 he accepted the challenge offered by another type of notable service and became President of the *New York Evening Post* for a period of four years, spending his energies and great abilities—during a postwar era of low standards in public trust and laxness in international obligations—for the promotion of an informed, honest, perceptive, and responsible citizenship. In 1924 he returned to Harvard as Professor of Economic History, and by his ever-generous gifts of companionship and counsel to those who worked under his direction, Dr. Gay endeared himself to still another generation of Harvard students. In this period he was also active as director of the National Bureau of Economic Research from 1924 to 1933, and in the work of the Council on Foreign Relations. He served the latter organization as secretary and treasurer for twelve years, as a director from 1921 to 1945, as chairman of its Research Committee, and as a member of the Editorial Advisory Board of *Foreign Affairs.*.

A short visit to the Huntington Library in the late summer of 1935 led Dr. Gay to appraise the resources offered here, particularly by the Stowe collection, for his long-standing investigations in the field of English economic history. In September, 1936, Dr. Gay exercised his option of retiring from the Harvard faculty as professor emeritus, in order to join the Research Group of the Huntington Library. Some five years later he assumed further responsibilities as Chairman of the group. Articles, concerned chiefly with the Temple family of Stowe in the seventeenth century, appeared from time to time in the *Quarterly*, mirroring the successive stages of his inquiry into these primary sources. A synthesis of his studies in the agrarian history of the sixteenth and seventeenth centuries, as well as a major work on the Industrial Revolution, remained incomplete at the time of his death—a death from pneumonia undoubtedly hastened by many months of anxiety over the health of the beloved wife who predeceased him by only a few weeks.

The colleagues, friends, and old students of Dr. Gay are scattered throughout the world. In their memory he lives as a man who honored wisdom and truth, who gladly learned, and would gladly teach. The careless, the inexact, the pretentious found no favor in his eyes. Without setting himself to preach the counsels of perfection, he so well practiced them that others kindled to the inspiration; he leaves behind him the reputation of one of Harvard's great teaching scholars. A humanist in the field of economic history, he buttressed the new academic study of business administration against outside pressures that might have debased its dignity. He also widened the arc of historical knowledge—although great modesty concerning his own erudition, joined to a passion for the highest standards, led him to publish comparatively little and leave in print nothing which quite does justice to the breadth of his learning or the height of his intellectual stature.

During the ten years that the Huntington Library knew Dr. Gay, its trustees and staff and readers came deeply to value him for the worth of his calm judgment, the quality of his friendship, and the hallmark of an integrity that was stamped upon all his deeds and thoughts.

The Gabriel Moraga Expedition of 1806:
The Diary of Fray Pedro Muñoz

THE old Mission of Santa Barbara is a great repository of manuscript records and other documents relating to the history of the Franciscan Order in California. In a recent co-operative undertaking between the Mission Archives and the Huntington Library, the latter institution undertook to film and photostat reproductions of these records for the twofold purpose of aiding the Mission in the preservation of its rare materials and of enabling the Library to add to its California collections. The work was financed by the grant from the Rockefeller Foundation to the Library for a study of the Southwest.

The Mission quite rightly reserves its official records for publication by its own historians, but Reverend Maynard Geiger, O.F.M., Franciscan historian and archivist at the Mission, has generously given permission to Huntington Library authorities to publish certain of these records of early California which have secular rather than ecclesiastical interest. The following document, translated by Miss Haydée Noya of the Library staff, is the first of such manuscript records to appear in the *Quarterly*.

Gabriel Moraga, leader of the expedition in question, was one of the most remarkable sons of the Spanish border. Coming to California as a boy in the second Anza expedition, he lived for a time at San Francisco where his father was the Presidio's first commandant.

Enlisting in the army, Moraga later distinguished himself both as soldier and explorer. According to Chapman, his service record in 1820 showed that he had taken part in forty-six expeditions against the Indians; and many California landmarks, including the San Joaquin, Sacramento, Merced, and Mariposa rivers, still bear the names he attached to them. His explorations covered the Sacramento Valley, as far north as the Feather River, many of the rivers that penetrate the Sierra Nevada Mountains, the Mojave and Colorado deserts, perhaps as far as Nevada, and especially the great valley of the San Joaquin.

One of Moraga's early expeditions into the San Joaquin, that of 1806, is described in the following document. The diarist, Fr. Pedro Muñoz, came to California in 1804 and after a brief stay at San Fernando was transferred to the Mission of San Miguel. He accompanied Moraga on the expedition for the threefold purpose of serving as diarist, selecting desirable sites for a chain of missions in the interior to parallel those along the coast, and baptizing as many heathen as God in His good providence would permit.

Muñoz gave a detailed and at times extraordinarily vivid description of the great valley, of its still wild and uncivilized tribes, and of the discomforts and hardships incident to the journey. His passion for the conversion of souls reached an intensity the modern mind cannot understand, but his zeal and sincerity must excite even the skeptic's admiration. Because of his passionate interest in the salvation of the Indians, his account of their enthusiastic acceptance of the Gospel and their eagerness for a mission is doubtless overdrawn.

Bancroft, Englehardt, Chapman, and other California historians of the period have made use either of the original Muñoz diary in the Santa Barbara Mission archives or of a transcript in the Bancroft Library at Berkeley. Bancroft printed a summary of the document as a footnote in Volume II of his *History of California*, and Englehardt in his *Missions and Missionaries of California* includes both a short description of the expedition and a brief day-by-day summary of the route.

ROBERT GLASS CLELAND

DIARY OF FR. PEDRO MUÑOZ

TRANSLATED BY HAYDÉE NOYA

Diary of the expedition led by Don Gabriel Moraga,[1] Lieutenant of the Company from San Francisco, to the new discoveries in the

[1]See preface. Three other expeditions visited the San Joaquin Valley in 1806. The most important of the three, probably led by Lieutenant Francisco Ruíz, left Santa Barbara on July 19. Father José María Zalvidea served as diarist and wrote a full account of the expedition. These and other expeditions into the San Joaquin

tular territories, by order of the governor, Don Josef Joaquín de Arrillaga.[2] The expedition was begun on the 21st of September, 1806.

The First Day—September 21st.

This morning the troop was formally addressed and informed of the task chosen for them by God in this expedition, and of the merit which would accrue to them if, following God's will through the voice of their leader, they should discharge their duties faithfully. Resigned and well-disposed, we left the Mission of San Juan Bautista[3] about two o'clock in the afternoon. We proceeded for about a league and a half bearing slightly to the east. By the middle of the afternoon we crossed a large plain covered with luxuriant grass and came to a creek called Huzaymas, the banks of which were well covered with elders, oaks, and other trees. This creek becomes dry during the summer and retains water only in scattered pools. It has a large bed and must be of considerable affluence during the rainy season. We camped here for the night, during which nothing happened worth recounting.

Second Day—The 22nd.

At daybreak the expedition got under way, with the inconveniences attendant upon a bad terrain. Having traveled eight leagues, we halted before a valley of tulares, previously explored by the expedition from the Presidio of San Francisco and by them named San Luis Gonzaga, because of its having been discovered on that

---

are described at some length in an unpublished thesis, submitted for the degree of Master of Arts at the University of California in 1919, by Miss Helen Papen. Translations of a number of the diaries of the expeditions, other than that of Father Muñoz, are included in the thesis. I am indebted to the Kern County Free Library of Bakersfield, California, for the privilege of consulting Miss Papen's manuscript. For the first expedition, that of Pedro Fages, into the southern part of the San Joaquin, see Herbert E. Bolton, "In the South San Joaquin Ahead of Garcés" (pamphlet, 1935).

[2] Governor of California from 1802 to 1814. Arrillaga also served as acting governor from 1792 to 1794.

[3] The mission, in what is now northern San Benito County, was founded by Father Lasuén in 1797.

saint's day.[4] It has a fairly large bubbling spring, which should prove sufficient for watering crops. This spring runs into the bed of a medium-sized stream, which was found dry and probably flows on the surface during the rainy season. The land in this vicinity is alkaline. During the night the troop had to endure three showers. Thus ends today's account.

Third Day—The 23d.

This morning we marched towards the east and, after traveling some six or eight leagues, came to a place previously discovered and named Sta. Rita. Here we pitched our camp, from which base we went out to examine the discoveries previously recorded. Prior to reaching this place we had found a large river bed, deep in places, but with water only in pools. This land contains saltpetre and is well covered with grass at this time of year. Numerous herds of deer and pronghorn antelopes may be seen all about. Sta. Rita itself has a creek, whose water situation is like that of the creek previously mentioned, except that, due to an excess of sand, the water here is still more scanty. This section of country also has great tulares, and the stream itself has an abundance of black willows.

Fourth Day—The 24th.

This morning our expedition moved southwardly (from our base camp) and we went in search of a rancheria which is said to have a population of four hundred. It was our misfortune to find no one in it, and in fact, to find but a few signs of its ever having been inhabited. Unable to discover where the population had gone, we proceeded east to explore a large river already discovered by the lieutenant, Don Gabriel, and named by him the San Joaquin.[5] This river is about two leagues from the camp at Sta. Rita. The river and surrounding territory must be impassable during the rainy season, for we found ample evidence of overflow of water all around. Along the course we followed there are two large river

[4]Probably San Luis Creek.

[5]Visited and named by Moraga sometime prior to 1806. Previously known as the San Francisco.

beds fed by the San Joaquin River. On all sides may be seen large tulares which probably become very swampy during the rainy season. From this river we returned to our camp, and so ended this day.

Fifth Day—The 25th.

Today we moved our camp to the above-mentioned river of San Joaquin. It has excellent meadows and fertile lands and very good pasture in the middle fields, although it has occasional patches of *tequesquite* [sodium carbonate] and saltpetre. We pitched our camp by the side of the river. According to the Indians of this territory, there is here an abundance of beaver and salmon. Forty-two armed Indians visited our camp this afternoon, demonstrating great affability and making us a present of fish. Showing to them an image of Our Lady of Dolores, I tried to explain to them the object of our coming, which afforded them great joy, and their behavior was such that it seemed as if they already were enlisted under the banner of the Holy Christ. Trusting to our good faith and friendliness, they stayed in our camp overnight, enjoying our efforts at hospitality and greatly admiring our clothes and beads.

Sixth Day—The 26th.

This morning we talked to the Indians who had remained with us, telling them of our desire to visit their village, and they offered to go with us as guides. With such safe conduct assured, we set out, reaching our destination after traveling some three leagues. The place was situated on the other side of the river, hidden behind some willows. It is called Nupchenche and has around 230 people under a chief named Choley. They gave us welcome as follows: A very old woman came forward to shower us with grain, followed by their captains who led us to the place prepared for the reception. Here they had spread some soft rush mats and deer hides upon which they served an abundance of dishes and two loaves of very white bread made with a grain resembling our rice.[6] After having eaten a sufficiency (they take it very ill if one refuses)

---

[6]According to Pedro Fages, the California Indians used three or four species of grain which he called rice.

I made known to them the object of our visit. They gave us a willing ear and, having heard the divine word in silence, requested to be made Christians. I baptized twenty-three old women and three old men. The rest of the Indians regretted very much that they were not also made Christians, but I told them my reasons, and they now await the coming of the mission to be led to heaven (may almighty God grant that it be so). They wished me to remain with them, but that being out of the question, I advised them ever to seek baptism and to disown their own heathenism, especially when in danger of death. All these lands are excellent and covered with grass. There is an abundance of ground cherries.

Seventh Day—The 27th.

This morning we crossed the river and, proceeding north, passed through a league of very high and thick *tules*, among which there were clear patches well covered with grass. After continuing on for some three leagues, we stopped at midday by a stream which runs from east to north and which had no running water, but only some pools. We were obliged to pitch our camp here. The lands between the tulares and this place are very unattractive. Beds of saltpetre and *tequesquite*, with an infinite amount of tulares, is all that can be seen. There are some sixty oaks and a few willows by this stream. Pasture land is very scarce, for besides having been evidently burned by the gentiles, it can be seen that the earth is poor and yields little grass. We named this place *Mariposas* [Butterflies] because these abounded, especially at night and during the morning.[7] These butterflies became quite a nuisance. Their eagerness to escape the sun's rays was so pronounced that they pursued us closely everywhere and one of them got inside the ear of one of the privates, causing him great discomfort and us much trouble in extracting it.

Eighth Day—The 28th.

Today, despite its being Sunday, we had to divide the expedition in three groups because, due to the scarcity of water and grass in

[7]The slough, river, and county are still called Mariposa.

our camp, we had to set out in quest of another site. One of the groups remained guarding the camp, and the second and third companies proceeded, one to the north and the other northeast. Both exploring parties discovered a large river with many Indians by its banks, all of whom fled at our approach. The lieutenant, however, was able to round up twelve of them, assuring them of our good will. The sergeant who had gone to the northeast rounded up eighteen more, but he was unable to win them over despite all his kindly demonstrations. Don Gabriel was informed of three other rancherias by the river, besides the one he was in, and where, according to the Indians, there were some 250 inhabitants. After locating several good camping and grazing sites, the groups turned and came back to the place of the butterflies, where the rest of the troop was waiting.

Ninth Day—The 29th.

On this day we set out very early towards the northeast. After traveling three leagues we came to the river discovered the day before. We named this river *Nuestra Señora de la Merced* (Our Lady of Mercy).[8] It has excellent banks, well peopled with Indians, as disclosed by the many wide and long trails along the lands bordering the river. We hope to find here a suitable place for the founding of a mission, for the flat lands are excellent and well covered with grass and oaks. Everything has to be examined and the results will be noted as we make the explorations. The waters of this river are excellent and very abundant—suitable for cattle-raising, farming, etc. The banks are heavily bordered with willows, ash-trees, cottonwoods, and *torote*. We came upon two rancherias, deserted because the inhabitants had become frightened on seeing our camp and had fled to the mountains. In one of them, however, we found an old Indian woman who had been unable to flee because of her very advanced years. When we tried to approach her, she drew strength out of her weak frame and gained the river, wading into a deep pool, from which we had to rescue her. One of our neophytes quickly stripped himself and waded in after her, having to draw her out against her will: she seemed to prefer the fury of

[8]The river flows through the Yosemite.

the waters to our company, despite our demonstrations of good will. When we had succeeded in pulling her out we tried to appease her fears with such tokens of good will as our conditions permitted. As soon as I noticed her to be more cheerful, I proceeded to teach her, offering her the Kingdom of God, and giving her as much instruction as was possible within the time available. I baptized her, upon which she gave tangible evidence of the joy that filled her heart. Treated affectionately as she was, when we gave her safe-conduct to depart, she did not wish to avail herself of it, declaring that she preferred to stay with us.

Tenth Day—The 30th.

Today part of the expedition proceeded to the northwest, discovering another river, similar in volume and clearness of its waters to the Merced, but running between high banks. Another party traveled upstream, to the east. This group came upon many Indians, no doubt from the three rancherias we had heard about. Near midday, we saw some Indians among the willows by the river and called to them with great affability, but they seemed very timid and did not dare leave their hide-outs. In the end, reassured by our demonstrations of good faith and friendliness, three of them came to us. We gave them food and I distributed a few trinkets among them, which seemed to put them at their ease. I told them how happy I would be if they brought their fellows. This they promised to do, and shortly afterwards came with thirty of them, explaining that the others were too frightened to come. This was the manner of their coming into our camp: on leaving the willows, they deposited their arms against a large oak and then, in double file, proceeded in good order to our camp, with one of them walking in the lead, whose office it was to call out to us. Our interpreter said these exclamations invited our friendship and the opportunity to show us the goodness of their hearts. Hearing these pleas, I ordered that food be prepared for them. After partaking of it they left, very happy, asking to be converted and baptized, for I had made known to them the goodness of God and the benefit intended for their souls. The Merced River has much wild vegetation. The Indians are hairless and somewhat stupid (*mesteños*). A cross was erected on this site; and so ended the day.

Eleventh Day—Oct. 1st.

Today the expedition followed a north-northwesterly direction, searching for the river we discovered yesterday. We reached it after marching some seven or eight leagues. It is a large river, similar to the one we named Our Lady of Merced. Its flow is banked high and it waters small meadows whose pastures are scanty due to alkaline deposits. We named this river Our Lady of Dolores, having discovered it in September on that day.[9] This river is bordered with bushes like those of the river mentioned before. No Indians were to be seen, but there were signs of several rancherias; no doubt the Indians from the other river must have come to inform these of our coming and they must have fled; this seemed to be so, judging from the long and wide trails they had left.

Twelfth Day—Oct. 2d.

This morning we continued in the same direction as yesterday. Having gone about a league, we discovered the bed of a large stream, full of sand and without water. It may well be a large river during the rains, snow, etc. It is bordered by oaks and some willows. From this stream we sighted a grove of oaks a short distance away and went towards it. We had to walk some two leagues to reach it. As we proceeded into it, it impressed us as having no end, but proved to be about four leagues wide; the length was too great for us to determine. Several varieties of oak are to be found in the mountains. There is little grass because of poor soil. After advancing for a league and a half, we came across another river, similar in size and clearness of water to the former ones, but running through a much deeper canyon. It is bordered by an abundance of wild grapes, a bit of *torote* and many ash trees. Here we pitched camp, and from our base proceeded to explore. We named this river Our Lady of Guadalupe.[10]

[9]Bancroft, Chapman, and Englehardt tentatively identify the Dolores as the Tuolumne.

[10]The Stanislaus.

Thirteenth Day—Oct. 3d.

This morning we set out along the river towards the east, and after a six-league march came to an Indian village called Taulamne.[11] This village is built on steep cliffs, inaccessible because of their sharp, dangerous rocks. The Indians live in caves; they go to and from these caves by the use of thin poles, which one Indian holds while the other slides down or climbs along it. We were not successful in prevailing upon them to come to the small meadow by the river where we were stationed near a pool. After we grew tired of offering them the things they usually like, while they persisted in their refusals, we decided to climb up on foot to where they were. For this step, we asked their permission, starting up only after they granted it, but were unable to reach them. Seeing that this was so, twelve or fifteen of them came down to a flat among the rocks, still distrustful and carrying their arms. However, again assured of our good will, they finally welcomed us. I gave them beads and *pinole*. They explained their stubborn refusals to come down by saying that they were afraid because soldiers killed and mishandled people. I passed at once to the object of our expedition, which was to offer them the Kingdom of God and our friendship, that their souls might be saved. They all answered that they wished to become Christians and asked for a mission. In spite of this willingness, it was impossible to baptize any one of them, even though there were many old women who imminently required baptism, because they refused to come down from their positions, and the climb was too difficult for me. They told us that there were six rancherias up the river, but we could not elicit from them even their own names or the name of their chief, so great was their fear, or perhaps their rascality. They are hairless and very dull. Judging their number by those we saw at different times among the rocks and trails, which hang like balconies over these precipices, this rancheria seemed to consist of about two hundred inhabitants. We returned to camp from here without any other occurrence, save that some Indians from the river chased a little neophyte Indian who was with us but had strayed from our party.

[11]The name of Tuolumne County, Tuolumne River, etc., probably comes from this village.

Fourteenth Day—Oct. 4th.

Today our progress was somewhat to the northwest. At a distance of about six leagues we came to a dry stream, well covered with ash trees and wild growths. We named it the San Francisco, since it was discovered on that saint's day. The expedition continued on, and at about nine leagues from the San Francisco, we came upon a large river which, we are informed, had been already discovered by an expedition seeking a land route to Bodega.[12] We found many gentiles by this river, who proved themselves both affectionate and affable. None were baptized because there was no interpreter, their language being entirely different from that of the tribes we had met previously. From the few words that were understandable, we gathered that they wanted a mission and to become Christians. The vicinity of this river has excellent land, suitable for planting and grazing, and is wooded with oak. There is pine in the sierra. The stream was called the Passion River by the expedition which discovered it. It has an abundance of ash trees, *torote*, wild onions, and willows. From here the expedition returned to the Guadalupe River, mentioned on the 12th day of our march, October the 2d, where our camp was located.

Fifteenth Day—Oct. 5th.

During the afternoon of this day, forty armed Indians suddenly made their appearance in our camp. They shot arrows into the air and performed ritualistic war-dances, after which three of them came forward in the capacity of ambassadors, bearing a flag made of a black band of feathers with a red stripe through its center. The whole camp was aroused and we received them with our arms at the ready. Seeing that both our arms and our numbers were superior to theirs, they addressed us more courteously than we had anticipated, merely asking if we had come to kill them, for they said they had been informed of such a purpose, and gave that as the reason for their great fright. Reassuring them of our good will by every means at our command, and declaring our intentions to

[12]Probably the Calaveras. The expedition "seeking a land route to Bodega" either must have come from one of the southern missions or wandered far afield.

be the opposite of what they had expected, we allowed one of them to carry the news to the rest of the Indians, who had remained near the river. Being thus informed, they approached closer on the opposite bank of the river, but it was not possible to persuade any of them to cross over to us. In the face of their stubbornness, we suggested to them that we cross to where they were. They agreed to this but as soon as we started they fled and were not ever seen again. The two who had remained with us were treated with utmost gentleness and affection, and permitted to leave the following morning.

Sixteenth Day—Oct. 6th.

Today we left our camp on the Guadalupe River and proceeded to the camping site on the Dolores, mentioned on the 11th day. Part of the expedition went by way of the sierra. It met many Indians, but did not find a suitable place for a mission—the land being poor, with little grass, etc., and the river highly banked.

Seventeenth Day—Oct. 7th.

Today the expedition moved from the Dolores to the Merced River mentioned on the 8th day. Part of the troop explored the sierra. It found many Indians close to the river. Their numbers could not be estimated because whenever they saw the troop approaching, they fled like the wind, and not wishing to use violence, our group was unable to talk to any of them. The balance of the expedition, which had gone by way of the fields and hillsides, found some twenty children by the river bank. These were so engrossed in their games that they did not see us until we had come upon them. Overcome by surprise, they began to yell and to escape by throwing themselves in the river, being so frightened and in such haste that they took many a bad fall. These mishaps included some of the older women, who were guarding them. They did not desist until they saw their men come out with their arms to defend them. We gave these men no attention, not wishing to frighten them, but did make some show of friendliness, and then left them, crossing to the other side of the river to pitch our camp in its excellent meadow. As soon as we dismounted, seventy-nine Indians, attracted by the novelty, came to us in good order, to pay us a visit, bringing us grain and fish. They showed themselves helpful and we became quite friendly with them. We welcomed them and gave them some beads, after which they retired to their rancheria on their own side of the river.

Eighteenth Day—Oct. 8th.

This morning we went over to the rancheria to pay them a visit in acknowledgment of their civility to us, carrying with us the standard of Our Holy Mary of Dolores, our patron saint. They received us with great joy, spreading out soft rush mats on the ground for us to sit upon. When these preliminaries were over, I made known to them the object of our visit. They answered with demonstrations of pleasure that they all wanted to be baptized and to have a mission. I baptized six old women and an old man. The majority of the women had fled upon our arrival, but estimating the population by the number of the men, this rancheria must be of about two hundred souls. It is called Latelate. There is another rancheria adjacent to this one, called Lachuo, which has about the same population. This is a good place in which to found a mission and a presidio. Its spacious meadows and excellent soil cannot be surpassed for crops, cattle, etc.

Nineteenth Day—Oct. 9th.

This morning the expedition started east and after advancing about eight leagues came to a spot full of small willows, by a dry stream which, however, had some pools of water. This place is at the foot of a hill, the top of which has some small, bushy oaks. This site is inconvenient because of its little grass. The trail followed today has abounded in pebbles and has, therefore, proved uncomfortable. We had found another dry stream about a league before reaching this place, with a large pool by a rock but no trees.

Twentieth Day—Oct. 10th.

The expedition continued today in the same direction, and after traveling some two leagues, we sighted a range covered with oaks and willows, and also the large bed of a stream which must carry abundant water in the rainy season, but now had only some pools of water and a bit of grass. Continuing on for three more leagues, we found a river, with from two to five stream beds, with water only in pools due to excess of sand. The banks have grass, willows, oaks, and ash trees. We spent the night here. An exploring party penetrated the side of the sierra, but found nothing worthy of notice. All the ground on our course today proved very poor in pastures, though rich in pebbles. Many of the pebbles are quartz and, judging from their beautiful appearance, are or seem to be rock crystals. The first of the streams we have mentioned, which we came to after our night's rest, is called the Santo Domingo. Our camp of today is called "Tecolote" [owl], because it abounds in this type of bird.

Twenty-first Day—Oct. 11th.

This morning we continued in the same eastward direction, and after a march of four leagues came to a stream well bordered with willows and oaks. It was dry, but had a large pool of water. We called it the Santa Ana. It is banked quite low on the side nearest the valley. We continued on our course and after four more leagues came upon the San Joaquin River, already mentioned in the fourth day of our march. All the land explored from the "Tecolote" to the Santa Ana is worse than bad, but from the Santa Ana to the San Joaquin there is some grass, although thin and lifeless. There are some stream channels but too indifferent for mention, though they may carry some water during the rainy season. From the Santa Ana to the San Joaquin the land is level and free of pebbles. The approaches to the sierra, and more so the sierra itself, are covered with oaks.

Twenty-second Day—October 12th.

Today the expedition rested, it being Sunday and the horses being very much in need of rest.

Twenty-third Day—October 13th.

This morning the expedition proceeded to explore and reconnoiter along the San Joaquin River. One section of the troop went downstream and the other upstream, by the sierra. The latter, in going further into the sierra, discovered an abundance of pine and redwood. They also found a rancheria of some two hundred souls, by the river bank, called Pizcache. The name of their chief is Supyucomu. This chief furnished our men with the following information, having been an eye-witness of these events: that some soldiers from the other side of the sierra (presumably from New Mexico) came here a good while back (about 20 years, by the Indians' reckoning), and that, the gentiles having attacked them, the soldiers gave battle, killing many of them;[13] that the gentiles had since remained in fear of the return of those soldiers, and now they saw that they had shown up from the other side of the sierra; that they, however, marveled at the kindness shown them when they had expected extermination. The chief added that on the other side of the sierra, to the north (judging from the signs he made), was the sea, and that it took them ten days to reach it; that towards the south there is no ocean, but a vastness of land spreading out in low hills; that the soldiers that had come before were in no way different from us in respect to horses, arms, and dress. This Indian, who affirms with signs the presence of the ocean, having himself been there, was in the fight with the soldiers. In the light of his evidence, we assume New Mexico to be very near on the other side of the sierra. In this rancheria four persons became Christians—two old men and two old women. From out the recesses of the sierra there issues a large river which branches off into two streams—one towards the other side of the sierra, and one towards this side, which is the San Joaquin we are exploring. The section of the troop that went downstream found only poor land, alkaline in places and with poor grass. Possibly a mission might be founded by this river because of its good meadows and abundance of timber, though

[13]No record of this expedition is known, but the circumstantial nature of the Indian account leads one to believe that such a record may some day come to light.

there is scarcity of firewood and grazing land. A cross was carved on an oak by the river, where the camp had been.

Twenty-fourth Day—October 14th.

Today we broke our camp on the San Joaquin River and continued in the same easterly direction. At a distance of five leagues we came upon the Santos Reyes River, discovered last year (1805).[14] The grazing lands here are indifferent, but the meadows by the river are excellent. All these meadows are well supplied with oaks, alder trees, ash trees, cottonwoods, and willows. The river abounds in beaver and fish. It is a suitable site for a mission, and perhaps also for a presidio. The land is excellent for farming, cattle-raising, etc. Today we also came upon a small rancheria, where, however, we only found two old women and a sick native, the rest of the inhabitants being abroad on their fields. We did not stop here because the clouds threatened rain. In fact, no sooner had we pitched camp and put up some tents than the rain began to pour at a furious pace.

Twenty-fifth Day—October 15th.

The expedition has been unable to venture out today because of torrential rain; the troop remained under cover waiting for the weather to clear that they might proceed with their exploration.

Twenty-sixth Day—October 16th.

The weather having cleared today, we left a few men to guard the camp and divided the rest of the troop into two groups—one to proceed upstream towards the sierra and the other downstream. The first group discovered a rancheria of about sixty people, under a chief named Achagua. Nine were made Christians, an old man and eight old women; all want a mission and wish to be baptized. The information gathered on the 23d day concerning the former passage of soldiers and the location of the ocean was here confirmed. Information was also gathered about six other rancherias, situated by the river bank near the sierra. The group which went

[14]Still known as the Kings River.

downstream discovered three rancherias containing altogether some three hundred people—the three being adjacent to one another and located on a spacious and lovely plain by the river. At the first of these rancherias fourteen of the natives became Christians — two old men and the rest old women. The name of their chief is Chaochay. At the second rancheria, although it was a large one, only one old woman was baptized, because as soon as the natives had spied us at the neighboring rancheria they had fled to the willow groves. The chief of this second rancheria is named Chayalate. At the third rancheria ten were converted, all of them old women. Their chief's name is Chatene. The sierra carries pine and redwood. Water is easily procurable. All these Indians have shown themselves very gentle; they want a mission and desire to be baptized.

Twenty-eighth Day—October 18th.

Today a small detachment of soldiers was sent out in search of water and grass. After a march of three or four leagues they found several waterholes in a large oak grove. The water is not very plentiful, but we decided to stop there tomorrow.

Twenty-ninth Day—October 19th.

The expedition proceeded today to the place discovered yesterday and went into the oak grove, finally stopping at the waterholes. We found the water somewhat stagnant, but since it was already late, we had no choice but to pitch our camp here. We visited a rancheria that has about six hundred people, twenty-two of whom became Christians. Their chief's name is Gucayh. We came upon other rancherias, but the people had vanished before we arrived. The number of converts given includes those baptized by the previous expedition.

Thirtieth Day—October 20th.

Finding the oak grove to be full of dry stream beds, we set out in search of their source. After traveling one league we came upon a large rancheria, all the inhabitants of which had hidden themselves among the neighboring willows. From here we proceeded eastwardly and, having covered a league and a half, found another rancheria called Cohochs, whose chief is named Chumucu. We were received with evident delight by this poor people. After we had made God and the good of their souls known to them, they wanted baptism and a mission. Following the direction of the sierra we found a fine river which had already been discovered by another expedition which came by here at the end of April of this year. It is dry due to an excess of sand and only during the rains and snows does it flow abundantly into all the streams of the oak grove; but water could be drawn up easily if a mission should be founded here. This oak grove, with its three thousand souls desirous of baptism and ministry, is the most suitable place for a mission of all those we have explored. There are excellent lands for cultivation, and good pastures in many sections of the oak grove which remain green at all times. There are also sizable spaces covered with saltpetre and *tequesquite.* This river is called the San Gabriel[15] and branches into another river which we called the San Miguel, the latter feeding various streams. This mission, should God grant its foundation, can have all kinds of timber—pine, redwood— and also good soil for cultivation. After examining all these things we returned to camp.

Thirty-first Day—Oct. 21st.

Today there was some reconnoitering towards the east where, after some seven leagues, we came to a river called the San Pedro[16] which had already been discovered in April by the previously mentioned expedition. Finding it without water along the part explored, we were forced to move our camp to the 600-soul rancheria mentioned before, called Telame,[17] which had good grass but very little water. Here we pitched camp.

[15]The San Gabriel was our modern Kaweah.

[16]Now known as the Tule. The large unnamed river south of the Tule was probably the Kern.

[17]In 1817 "the place called Telamé" was said, by Fr. Mariano Payeras, to have a population of 4,000 souls, and abundant grass and good land. See George W. Beattie, *California's Unbuilt Mission* (1930), p. 17.

Thirty-second Day—Oct. 22d.

Today, after reconnoitering all the sites and rancherias in the oak grove, the expedition rested while awaiting supplies from the San Miguel Mission.[18]

Thirty-third Day—Oct. 23d.

This morning I went with the Commandant, Don Gabriel Moraga, to the above-named rancheria of Telame. We had the good fortune to find there a little girl in a condition of wasting flesh and dying, whose parents gave her to me to baptize when I told them the good that was in store for her should she die a Christian. As soon as I baptized her, her parents showed great satisfaction at her good fortune, and we also because we had saved her soul. During the days we have stayed in this place, the Indians have proved themselves delighted with our company, to the point of showing us the site most suitable for the founding of a mission. All of the inhabitants of this rancheria have come to visit us—even though they had hidden themselves upon our arrival—and now bring us of their scanty possessions, and feel hurt if they are not accepted.

Thirty-fourth Day—October 24th.

There was nothing worth recording today, save that the supplies that were expected arrived during the early evening (*cuarto de prima*).

Thirty-fifth Day—October 25th.

This morning the supplies were distributed to the troop and, in the afternoon, we got on the march. We traveled east for about two leagues (guided by two gentiles) and then turned west. Two leagues further we came to a spring with abundance of water. To find this spring one must follow a large stream-bed to the east of the rancheria and then turn west, a distance of some four leagues all told. We supposed this water to be a seepage from the San Gabriel River through the sandy ground. The spring is well covered with grass, but the soil is mainly alkaline.

[18]The mission in northern San Luis Obispo County, across the Coast Range Mountains from the Tulares, was built in 1797.

Thirty-sixth Day—October 26th.

This afternoon we broke camp and crossed to an oak grove through which flows the San Pedro River, discovered by the expedition of April of this year—1806. We traveled about eight leagues—four towards the oak grove and four more through it to the east—where we found a river without water due to its thickness of willows, cottonwoods, *torote*, and ash trees, and also because of an abundance of sand. The river from here towards the sierra will be found to have enough water to support a mission. At the sierra it has good water, excellent fields for cultivation, sufficiency of grass, etc. There is a great deal of pine and redwood in the sierra.

Thirty-seventh Day—October 27th.

Today, as we traveled upstream, we came upon a small rancheria called Coyehete, at a distance of about a league; according to the information gathered from the gentiles it has four hundred souls. There was no one we could baptize, because although they wish it and want a mission, they are young. From this rancheria we struck to the east and at a distance of about a league found a stream called San Cayetano, discovered the same year as the preceding river. It was dry, but had many large waterholes, enough for any number of cattle. This river has an abundance of willow trees and some oaks, but its lands are not sufficiently fertile. Continuing east, another stream is found four leagues farther, full during the rains but dry at this time; it has, however, some willows. From here we followed a rivulet along which we traveled most of the day, finding it very long, and at sunset met a large stream with plenty of willows and an excess of sand. It being very late, we searched diligently for water, but without success. We began to dig into the sand and at a depth of about two *varas*[19] found water, but only enough for the troop, and unpalatable. The horses were very thirsty, having had no water since morning, but we had to hold them without drink until we might reach a river of abundant waters we were seeking, which had been discovered by an expedition sent this year from

[19]The hole was about 5½ feet deep.

the presidio of Santa Barbara.[20] We had to spend the night by this stream, finding nothing new to report except an excess of cold.

Thirty-eighth Day—October 28th.

The expedition set out very early this morning, and after some three leagues, came upon the river which I mentioned yesterday, discovered by the expedition from Santa Barbara. Its waters are abundant even during the dry season. All the lands explored today have been quite the poorest we have yet come across during our journey. There is some chamise and an abundance of *tuseros*— that is all the land contains. No grass of any kind, not even near the river, where we only found willows and saltpetre beds with *tequesquite*. While traveling downstream in search of grass we found the tracks of the horses from the Santa Barbara expedition. And having already traveled our limit for this day, we were forced to stop, even though the grass was scarce, in the immense willow grove by the river—willows and cottonwoods being the only growths found here in abundance.

Thirty-ninth Day—October 29th.

Today, after searching for grass, we moved our camp some three leagues down, where we had found a good deal of grass about a league from the river—though the ground itself was alkaline and with much chamise. The searching party went on towards the sierra and to the end of the plain, but found only saltpetre beds, *tequesquite*, and arid land.

Fortieth Day—October 30th.

The expedition remained inactive today to give the horses a rest already overdue.

Forty-first Day—October 31st.

Today we traveled towards a pass in the sierra through which we meant to cross, to bring our expedition to an end. On our way we found a rancheria about three leagues from camp. Here we

[20]The Ruíz-Zalvidea expedition mentioned in Note 1.

detached the lagging horses from our main body, that they might follow an easier route and be able to recuperate more readily. We are not reporting concerning this and another rancheria we saw by the river, judging that the Santa Barbara expedition has already done so in full. At sunset we reached the pass. Here we found abundance of running water in a small stream, and a great deal of wild grapes, which are almost its only vegetation. We spent the night here, although there was little grass for the horses.

Forty-second Day—November 1st.

Today we proceeded through the pass and after two leagues came to the source of the stream alongside of which we had slept. This source was a marsh, well covered with grass. This pass progresses along a sort of canyon covered with oaks, at the end of which is a lagoon entirely alkaline. To the east there is a fair-sized rancheria, the Indians of which proved thoroughly crafty and mercenary. Following the information of three gentiles from this rancheria, we reached another quite similar to it, but very much hidden among ravines and arid lands. It was not possible to estimate the population because they were celebrating at a neighboring rancheria. We continued east and came, after sunset, to a causeway holding a small stream of scanty water which was very brackish due to abundance of saltpetre on the stream bed.

Forty-third and last day of the expedition—November 2d.

Today, proceeding down the causeway, we came upon the ranch of the reverend fathers of the San Fernando Mission. The mountains we crossed today are indescribably rugged, but God allowed us to glimpse a light in the early evening, and directing our steps toward it we arrived at the ranch already mentioned. Next day we proceeded from here to the Mission.[21]

Whatever has been recorded in this diary represents what I myself have seen. The number of those baptized by me during the expedition, together with those previously baptized by the expedi-

---

[21]From the Santa Clara River the expedition crossed the steep, brush-covered Santa Susanna Range, which Muñoz well characterizes as "indescribably rugged."

tion of April of this year, 1806, is 141,—all of them baptized under extreme urgency. In testimony of the foregoing, I sign this on the 2d day of November, 1806.

Fr. Pedro Muñoz.

* * * * *

Here follows the number of rancherias inspected during this expedition, the number of their inhabitants, and the number of persons I baptized, reckoned together with those baptized during the expedition of April of this year, 1806.

Nupchenche

This rancheria consists of about 250 souls. Twenty-eight were baptized, — five old men and twenty-three old women....... 28

Chineguis

Population about equal to the preceding rancheria. An old woman was baptized 1

Yunate

By the usual way of computing, this rancheria has about the same number of persons as the preceding one. An old man was baptized 1

Chamuasi

Has about the same number of persons as the above rancheria. None were baptized because they had hidden themselves upon our arrival.

Latelate

This rancheria has about two hundred souls. I baptized six old women 6

Lachuo

In numbers, much like the preceding one. The same thing happened as in Chamuasi,—for which reason there was no one about to whom I might administer holy baptism.

Pizcache
This rancheria has in the neighborhood of two hundred souls.
Four were baptized,—two old men and two old women...... 4

Aycuyche
Has about sixty souls. Nine were made Christians—one old
man and eight old women............................ 9
Hereabouts there are six other rancherias which we did not
get to inspect, but according to the Indians of this rancheria,
the others are about the size of Pizcache.

Cesaa
This rancheria has about one hundred souls. Fourteen were
made Christians — two men and twelve women, all old, and
one of the women in a dying condition................. 14

Chiaja
This rancheria has about the same population as the preceding
one. An old woman was baptized..................... 1

Aayuase
Like the preceding one, it has about one hundred people. Nine
old women were baptized............................ 9

Capatau
This is a small rancheria under the jurisdiction of the chief of
the preceding one. It has from nine to twelve persons. One old
woman was baptized................................. 1

Hualo Vual
Has about four hundred souls. Two old women were baptized.
This rancheria was visited by the previous expedition........ 2

Tunctache

This rancheria has about 250 souls. One sick old man was baptized   1

Notonto No. 1

Ten persons were baptized in this rancheria,—eight old women and two dying children. They were baptized during the first expedition, and we found that the two children had subsequently died. This rancheria has about three hundred souls..   10

Notonto No. 2

Has about one hundred souls. Two old women were baptized   2

Telame No. 1

This is the largest of all the rancherias visited. According to a conservative estimate, it has about six hundred souls. It was inspected during the first expedition, when eleven old women and a dying man were baptized; we found the latter to have died. We baptized eight old women, one old man, and a dying little girl—twenty-two altogether........................   22

Telame No. 2

Has about two hundred souls. (Was not inspected during the previous expedition.) Six old women were baptized........   6

Vholasi

This rancheria has probably about one hundred souls. It was inspected during the first expedition. I baptized three old women   3

Cagueya

This is a rancheria of about three hundred souls, inspected during the first expedition. Ten were baptized—nine old women and a dying man, whom we found to have died later..   10

Cohochs

Has about one hundred souls. Eleven old women were baptized 11

Choynoque

This rancheria has about three hundred souls. None were baptized because fright had caused them to flee. The armed men who visited us led us to estimate this rancheria as having three hundred persons.

Cutucho

This rancheria is adjacent to the very first one we mentioned, called Nupchenche; it has about four hundred souls. It was inspected by the first expedition. None were baptized because they had fled.

Tahualamne

This rancheria has about two hundred souls. None were baptized because fright prevented them from coming down from their precariously perched habitations—as recorded on the 13th day of this diary (Nov. 3d).

Total of those baptized during both expeditions.......... 141

Coyehete

According to information received from the Indians, this rancheria has about four hundred souls. It has not yet been visited. There are many other rancherias which I am not mentioning for the same reason, because they have not as yet been inspected.

Fr. Pedro Muñoz.

English Metrical Psalms in the Sixteenth Century and their Literary Significance

By Hallett Smith

I

THE HISTORY of the development of Elizabethan poetry would hardly be complete without some account of the vogue, in the mid-century and later, of translating the Psalms into English verse. The curious reader will not find a very comprehensive account in the usual literary histories, and what he does find will be largely derived from Thomas Warton.[1] In a dignified eighteenth-century way, Warton scoffs at the Sternhold-Hopkins version of the Psalms and is amused and tolerant at the others. It must be confessed that some of his jibes are justified, but his description of the Psalm-translating movement is narrow in scope and often mistaken in fact. Considerable scholarly work has been done on early English psalmody by historians of music and by reverend antiquarians interested in tracing the development of the Protestant liturgy,[2] but these researches have had small influence upon the treatment of the Psalm translations by historians of English poetry. Twenty-five years ago Professor A.W. Reed[3] pointed out that a most important question about the development of English poetry in the sixteenth century could only be answered after a full consideration of the metrical versions of the Psalms. Yet no such full treatment has ap-

[1] *The History of English Poetry* (1824), III, 449-61.

[2] Besides John Julian, *A Dictionary of Hymnology* (revised edition, 1907), and the older J. Holland, *Psalmists of Britain* (1843), which *The Cambridge Bibliography of English Literature* cites as the primary authorities, the student of this subject should see the preliminary dissertations in Neil Livingston, *The Scottish Metrical Psalter of A. D. 1635* (Glasgow, 1864), and the learned and interesting recent book by Professor Waldo Selden Pratt, *The Music of the French Psalter of 1562* (New York, 1939). The information contained in Julian is vast in extent, but it is scattered, not always consistent, and now in need of correction. See Old Version, pp. 857 ff.; Psalters, English, pp. 916 ff.; Appendix I, pp. 1528-1542; Appendix II, p. 1684; English Hymnody, pp. 343 ff.; and the various articles under names of the translators.

[3] *The Year's Work in English Studies, 1920-21,* p. 57, reviewing Berdan's *Early Tudor Poetry.*

peared. It seems desirable, therefore, to re-examine the whole subject, considering the motives for metrical Psalm translation, noticing the background in the pre-Elizabethan period, and observing the results in four or five representative translations.

For a convenient summary of the attitudes toward the Old Version, as the work of Sternhold, Hopkins, and their collaborators used to be called, we may turn to Thomas Fuller. He says that the translators were "men whose piety was better than their poetry; and they had drank more of Jordan than of Helicon. These psalms were therefore translated to make them more portable in people's memories (verse being twice as light as the selfsame bulk in prose)." As for the critical reception of their efforts, "later men have vented their just exceptions against the baldness of the translation; so that sometimes they make the Maker of the tongue to speak little better than barbarism, and have in many verses such poor rhyme that two hammers on a smith's anvil would make better music; whilst others, rather to excuse it than defend it, do plead that English poetry was then in the nonage, not to say infancy thereof; and that, match these verses for their age, they shall go abreast with the best poems of those times. Some, in favour of the translators, allege that to be curious therein and over-descanting with wit had not become the plain song and simplicity of an holy style. But these must know there is great difference between painting a face and not washing it."[4]

Fuller skips rather lightly over the motives for verse translation, though he does recognize that piety often directed the poet's efforts and that facility of memorization was important. For him, however, the motives do not matter much; bad poetry is bad poetry, and no attempt to explain the purpose alters the quality of it.

Anthony à Wood contributes a further reason for the versification of the Psalms in English. In his account of Sternhold in *Athenae Oxonienses* he remarks that his author "was in some esteem in the Royal Court for his grave vein in Poetry, and other trivial learning. But being a most zealous Reformer; and a very strict liver, he became so scandaliz'd at the amorous and obscene Songs used in the Court, that he forsooth turn'd into English meeter 51 of *Davids*

[4]*The Church History of Britain*, ed. J. S. Brewer (Oxford, 1845), IV, 73-74.

Psalms, and caused musical notes to be set to them, thinking thereby that the Courtiers would sing them instead of their sonnets, but [they] did not, only some few excepted."[5]

Wood's remarks have been accepted as truth, and authorities like Mrs. C. C. Stopes[6] have expanded them in such a way as to present a picture of a rather absurd campaign on the part of Sternhold to turn the courtiers of Edward VI overnight into zealous puritans, intuning in the nose full seemly these homely Psalms. The campaign, Wood notes, failed with the courtiers, but resulted in an unexpected and extraordinary success with a larger audience, for, he says, "the Poetry and Musick being admirable, and the best that was made and composed in those times, they were thought fit afterwards to be sung in all Parochial Churches, as they do yet continue [1691]."[7] *The Short-Title Catalogue* lists 280 editions of Sternhold and Hopkins down to 1640, exclusive of the Scottish psalters, which also contained many Old Version Psalms. It is perhaps fair to say that no English verse whatever was so familiar to English ears in the second half of the sixteenth century as the "Common Meter" of this translation.

A view of this whole phenomenon more nearly accurate and objective than can be secured from Wood, Fuller, or Warton (or their modern derivatives) demands first of all an examination of the motives of the English translators in turning the Psalms into English verse. The movement is of course part of the Reformation, and as such involves the making of the scriptures accessible to the people in the vulgar tongue. But why in verse? The Psalms were largely available in English, through the medium of Primers or Books of Hours, in the reign of Henry VIII and even through that of Mary. But although the hymns in some of these primers were in verse, the Psalms were given in prose. The first reason for versify-

[5] *Athenae Oxonienses,* 1691, cols. 62-63, art. 82.

[6] "The Metrical Psalms and 'The Court of Venus,'" *Athenaeum* (June 24, 1899), pp. 784-86; *William Hunnis and the Revels of the Chapel Royal,* Bang's *Materialen,* Vol. 29 (1910), chap. i and note on pp. 285-86; *Shakespeare's Industry* (1916), pp. 291-333. Mrs. Stopes follows Warton, who followed Anthony à Wood. Had the tradition been based upon Strype, who gives an account in *Ecclesiastical Memorials,* Part II, Book I, chap. xi, it would have been much less misleading.

[7] *Loc. cit.*

ing the Psalms is, of course, that the learned, and perhaps some others, knew that in the original Hebrew the Psalms are poetry.[8] No prose rendering can effectually disguise that fact. Verse, then, as the proper medium for poetry, would seem to be the most suitable and natural medium for the Psalms. These songs, composed and sung to the harp by the foremost musician among the Hebrews (for David was accounted the author of all the Psalms), might be brought to life again—as poetry and as a form of worship[9]—if turned into verse the people understood.

Commentaries on the Psalms, even those which are concerned primarily with the content and not with the style, had to deal with the figurative language used by David, and sometimes even with the structure of the sentences. John Calvin, for example, encounters the problem directly and immediately; if the doctrine of the Psalms is to be made clear (and Calvin felt that the doctrine contained in the Psalms was a kind of *summa* of Christianity) the figures of speech and the language must be analyzed. When he comments on the familiar verses at the end of the 121st Psalm, which read, in the version he uses, "The Sonne shall not burne thee by day, nor the Moone by night. The Lord will keep thee from all evil, he wil keep thy Soule. The Lord wil harken to thy going out, and to thy coming in, from this time forth for evermore," Calvin explains as follows:

By these formes of speeche hee commendeth the frute of Gods presence: & by the figure Sinecdoche, under one perticuler, hee assureth the

[8]For a survey of critical opinion on this point, see Israel Baroway, "The Bible as Poetry in the English Renaissance: An Introduction," *Journal of English and Germanic Philology*, XXXII (1933), 447-80.

[9]The act authorizing the first prayer book of Edward VI (1549) made it lawful to "use openly" any Psalm or prayer taken out of the Bible. The 49th Injunction of Elizabeth, June, 1559, gave similar authorization. Strype quotes from a contemporary diary to show that psalm-singing "after the Geneva fashion; all the congregation, men, women and boys, singing together" was a novelty when it was introduced at St. Antholin's in September, 1559. (*Annals* [1824 ed.], Vol. I, Part I, p. 199.) Whittingham relates that the introduction of psalm-singing in the new order of worship drawn up by the exiles at Frankfurt in 1554 was following the custom "in the frenche dutche Italian Spanishe and Skottishe churches." (*A Brieff discours off the troubles begonne at Franckford . . .* [1575], sig. B[r]. See also the account in G. Burnet, *The History of the Reformation of the Church of England*, ed. N. Pocock (Oxford, 1865), II, 177-78.

faithful that they shalbe safe from all adversities, bicause they bee
sheelded with Gods hand. Neverthelesse there is in it a Metaphor also:
for by the colde of the night and the heate of the daye, the Prophete
betokeneth any maner of inconvenience.[10]

Calvin is careful, however, not to let his readers suppose that the
poetry in the Psalms is mere art; the Psalms are spiritual documents,
and since they are inspired by the Holy Ghost they must have in
them essential material designed primarily not for our entertain-
ment but for our profit. "Now forasmuch as it is certeyn," he says,
"that David boroweth not colored Rhetorik from the court barre,
wherewith to winne himselfe GODS favour: but rather takes his
reasons out of Gods woord: the sentences which he gathereth too-
gither heere for the strengthening of his fayth, must bee applyed
to our use."[11]

Englishmen who furthered the project of translating the Psalms
into English meter were well prepared with justifications. The
author of the preface to *The Forme of prayers, and Ministration
of the Sacraments, &c, used in the Englishe Congregation at Geneva . . . 1556*[12] (probably Whittingham) says:

. . . there are no songes more meete, then the psalmes of the Prophete
David, which the holy ghoste hath framed to the same use, and com-
mended to the churche, as conteininge the effect of the whole scriptures,
that hereby our heartes might be more lyvelie touched, as appereth by
Moses, Ezechias, Judith, Debora, Marie, Zacharie and others, who by
songes and metre, rather then in their commune speache, and prose, gave
thankes to god, for suche comfort as he sent them. Here it were to
longe to intreate of the metre. but for asmuche as the learned dout not
therof. and it is playnly proven that the psalmes are not only metre, and
conteyne juste Cesures: but also have grace and majestie in the verse
more then any other places of the scriptures, we nede not to enter into
any probation. For they that are skilfull in the hebrewe tounge by
comparinge the psalmes with the reste of the scriptures easelie may
perceyve the metre.

[10]*The Psalmes of David and others. With M. John Calvins commentaries* [tr.
Arthur Golding] (1571), sig. Bbbb2v. In quotations throughout the article type
peculiarities such as *u* for *v, i* for *j* have been modernized.

[11]Sig. T7v-T8r. Calvin gives his justification of psalm-singing, and a warning
against being more intent upon the music than the words, in *Institutes of the
Christian Religion*, Book III, chap. xx, sec. 32.

[12]STC 16561. Sig. B2v-B4r.

The second great reason alleged for the turning of the Psalms into English meter is the ease of memorizing. This pedagogical device was not the invention of the translators, but was attributed by them to the Holy Ghost itself: "to whome is it not knowen, how the holy ghoste by all meanes soght to helpe our memorie, when he facioned many psalmes according to the lettres of the Alphabet: so that every verse beginneth with the lettres thereof in ordre?"[13] Some of the learned and ingenious translators (Matthew Parker, for example) imitated this feature of the original Hebrew, but others, like Sternhold and Hopkins, contented themselves with aiding the memory by meter and rhyme.

For this purpose, a ballad stanza was chosen, perhaps as the usual meter associated with memorized poems, perhaps also because of its simplicity, regularity, and emphatic beat. This stanza, which consists of alternate lines of four beats and three beats, may also be considered a couplet of seven beats to the line. It is the most common of verse forms in the popular ballad, according to Gerould,[14] who counted 179 out of the 305 specimens in Child's collection as having this meter. Whether the form is really a seven-foot couplet in the ballads or not, in the Psalm versions it usually has a syntactical break or a strong enough pause at the end of the fourth foot to make it a separate line, so the form is best described as a 4.3.4.3 stanza.

The Common Meter used by the Psalm translators is predominantly, almost exclusively, iambic, and this fact, as Professor Reed has suggested, may have been of significance in the great change in the mid-sixteenth century from somewhat loose, syllabic versification, Skeltonics, and degenerated accentual alliterative poetry to the prevailing Elizabethan iambic manner first prominent in *Tottel's Miscellany*. Why the Psalm translations in Common Meter are so uniformly iambic it is not possible to say with complete confidence, but some suggestions may be made. In taking over a ballad stanza, the translators were forced to regularize somewhat, to elim-

---

[13] *Ibid.*

[14] G. H. Gerould, *The Ballad of Tradition* (Oxford, 1932), p. 126. For a discussion of this meter, see J. W. Hendren, *A Study of Ballad Rhythm* (Princeton, 1936), chaps. iv and v.

inate characteristic ballad anacrusis, and to simplify. There is plenty of evidence that they thought of one syllable, and one only, to a note of music. The occasional skipping movement of the ballad, or the freedom with which several syllables were covered by a single note of music, was impossible. It would be too difficult for non-musical members of the congregation to sing, and much more difficult to remember. There must have been something deliberate, however, in the choice of iambic, for the hymns in the Primers of Henry VIII are predominantly trochaic.

The success of Common Meter as a medium for the Psalms did show that the fourteener or 4.3.4.3 stanza was effective and easy to memorize. I have not been able to locate a book by I. or J. L. called *A good help for a weak memory, or the sum of the Bible in verse*, which Ritson notes in his catalogue,[15] but I strongly suspect it was in Common Meter, or, as it came to be called in the 1560's, Sternhold's meter. But I can point to another book (*STC* 3044 and 21690, which should have been listed under the same entry) by William Samuel, Minister, called *An Abridgement of all the Canonical Books of the Old Testament, written in Sternhold's meter...* (1569). Since the sole purpose of this book is memorization, and since "Sternhold's meter" is specified on the title page, it would seem that Common Meter was felt to be the appropriate verse form for anything which was to be memorized. Samuel offers a system whereby anyone who has memorized his book can tell, by counting up on the joints of his fingers, in exactly what book and chapter of the Bible any given story or parable is to be found. The book even contains an illustration showing a human hand, with the joints numbered and lettered, to make the system fool-proof.

The final reason for the versification of the Psalms in English is to compete with the profane lyrics of the courtiers, and no part of the history of mid-sixteenth-century English verse so much needs fresh treatment as this. Anthony à Wood, in the passage already quoted, shows a certain dry amusement at the project of trying to persuade courtiers to give up their gay songs and sing Psalms instead. It would seem absurd, on the face of it, and it becomes more so when we consider the verse form used (not French or Italian forms such

15[Joseph Ritson], *Bibliographia Poetica* (London, 1802), p. 265.

as Wyatt and Surrey had been experimenting with, but the homely beat of the ballad) and the general style. There is such a thing as spiritualizing profane songs, of course, and alleged success at doing so can be traced far back into the middle ages. Moreover, there is the example of Clément Marot, who in the 1530's had succeeded in creating a rage for his French versions of the Psalms in the French court, but paid for it by having to flee to Geneva. Marot's Psalms, although they became the standard French version, were not at first intended for wide popular singing; the variety of meters alone would prove that. They aimed at the court audience, and the manner in which they were made showed an appeal to a cultivated and sophisticated literary taste. Pratt has counted the verse forms or "meters" of the final form of the French Psalter (1562) and records the fact that there are 110 different "meters," each requiring a different kind of tune.[16] Are we to believe that Sternhold, who was himself a groom of the robes to Henry VIII and Edward VI, knew so little about the tastes of English courtiers that he thought they could be persuaded to sing Psalms instead of love-songs even when those Psalms were all done in the monotonous uniformity and simplicity of the ballad stanza?

As a matter of fact, there is no evidence from Sternhold himself that he had any such motive. The first edition of his Psalms, and the only one issued in his lifetime, contains a dedication to King Edward VI which gives the only authoritative account of Sternhold's purpose. The relevant passage is as follows:[17]

Seyng furdre that youre tender and godlye zeale doeth more delyght in the holy songes of veritie than in any fayned rymes of vanitie, I am encouraged to travayle furder in the sayed boke of psalmes, trustyng that as your grace taketh pleasure to heare them song sumtimes of me, so ye wil also delight not onely to se & read them your selfe, but also to commaund them to be song to you of others, that as ye have the Psalme it selfe in youre mynde, so ye maye judge myne endevoure by your eare.

There is nothing here about converting the courtiers by means of the Psalms, only praise of the boy King's sober and religious temper and an interest in having the King free to judge the music

[16]*Op. cit.*, p. 26.
[17]*STC* 2419 + (HN). Sig. A3r.

for its own sake. Apparently this taste on the King's part was genuine, because Dr. Christopher Tye, a musician of his chapel, dedicated to him a version of the book of Acts translated in the same meter Sternhold had used. Tye says, in his verse dedication, that others had pleased the King by undertaking to present the Psalms in rhyme, and still others had versified the book of Kings,[18]

> Because they se, your grace delyte
> Insuche like Godlye thynges.

If, as the *Dictionary of National Biography* suggests, Sternhold and Tye were the musical tutors of the King, their method seems to have been to provide their royal pupil with things they thought he would like, and then publish what had suited his taste.

Where did Anthony à Wood get the idea that Sternhold was trying to convert the courtiers to singing his Psalms? The answer may be twofold: that he saw not the first edition, which contains Sternhold's own account of what he was doing, but a later edition, published after the author's death, such as that of 1564[19] "by Thomas Sternhold and others" which is described on the title page as "Very meete to be used of all sortes of people privatly for their godly solace & comfort, laying aparte al ungodly songes & balades, whych tend only to the nourishyng of vyce and corruptyng of youth," and secondly that he may have confused Sternhold with Dr. John Hall, a violent crusader against courtly songs about 1550. There was good reason for confusing Sternhold and Dr. Hall, in that one of Hall's volumes, a translation of part of the book of Proverbs, was attributed to Sternhold on the title page of the first edition.[20]

As a matter of fact, the attack upon courtly songs in the name of

---

[18]*STC* 2984. Sig. A2ᵛ

[19]*STC* 2433.

[20]*STC* 2760. Hall reclaims the translation on the title page of *STC* 12631: *Certayn chapters taken out of the prouerbes/of Salomō, wyth other chapters/of the holy Scripture, & certayne/Psalmes of Dauid, translated/into English metre, by John Hall, Whych Prouerbes of late were set forth,/Imprinted and vn-/truely entituled, / to be thee do- / ynges of / May- / ster / Thomas Sternhold, late / grome of the Kynges / Maiesties robes, as / by thys Copye it / maye be per-/ ceaued. / M. D. L./*

the Psalms had been going on long before Sternhold or Hall either.
The earlier translators of the Psalms into English verse, Coverdale,
Becon, Wisdom, and Wedderburn, were under the influence of the
Lutheran movement, and they represent a zealous desire to substitute godly songs for all kinds of profane poetry. The extent to
which this program was carried by the preachers will hardly be
believed without illustration. Take Coverdale, for example:

O that men's lips were so opened, that their mouths might shew the
praise of God! Yea, would God that our minstrels had none other thing
to play upon, neither our carters and ploughmen other thing to
whistle upon, save psalms, hymns, and such godly songs as David is
occupied withal! And if women, sitting at their rocks, or spinning at
the wheels, had none other songs to pass their time withal, than such as
Moses' sister, Glehana's wife, Debora, and Mary the mother of Christ,
have sung before them, they should be better occupied than with
hey nony nony, hey troly loly and such like phantasies. . . . Seeing then
that, as the prophet David saith, it is so good and pleasant a thing to
praise the Lord, and so expedient for us to be thankful; therefore, to
give our youth of England some occasion to change their foul and corrupt ballads into sweet songs and spiritual hymns of God's honour, and
for their own consolation in him, I have here, good reader, set out
certain comfortable songs grounded on God's word, and taken some
out of the holy scripture, specially out of the Psalms of David, all
whom would God that our musicians would learn to make their songs!
and if they which are disposed to be merry, would in their mirth
follow the counsel of St Paul and St James, and not to pass their time
in naughty songs of fleshly love and wantonness, but with singing of
Psalms, and such songs as edify, and corrupt not men's conversation.
As for the common sort of ballads which are now used in the world,
I report me to every good man's conscience, what wicked fruits they
bring. Corrupt they not the manners of young persons? Do they not
tangle them in the snares of uncleanness? Yes, truly, and blind so the
eyes of their understanding, that they can neither think well in their
hearts, nor outwardly enter into the way of godly and virtuous living.
I need not rehearse, what evil ensamples of idleness, corrupt talking,
and all such vices as follow the same, are given to young people through
such unchristian songs. Alas! the world is all so full of vicious and
evil livers already, it is no need to cast oil in the fire. Our own nature
provoketh us to vices, God knoweth, all-to sore: no man needed en-
ticing thereto.[21]

[21]*Remains of Myles Coverdale*, ed. G. Pearson (Parker Society, 1846), pp. 537-38.

Or, with a somewhat more elevated rhetoric, the opinions of Thomas Becon:

What song may be compared unto thys our song? What Harpe maketh so goodly & pleasaunt melody, as this Harpe of David doth? Let al minstrels geve place to this our Minstrell. Let al Harpes & other musical instruments be silent and hold their peace, whan Davids harpe entreth and commeth in place. Let al songes be banished, whan Davids Psalmes be song. For whatsoever David singeth, it is excellent and incomparable. He wyth his songs exciteth, provoketh and enflameth the mynds of the faythfull and dilygent hearers unto the love and desyre not of transitory but of heavenly thynges. He comforteth the comfortles. He exhorteth the synner unto amendement of lyfe. He lifteth up the desperate unto the hope of gods mercy. He corroborateth and maketh strong the weake. He healeth the diseased. He rayseth up the dead unto lyfe. He maketh the sad mery. He exhilarateth and rejoyseth the merely [merrily] disposed. To conclude, he is a Mynstrel fit for al kind of persons, so that they be bent unto godlynes. Ah would God that al Minstrels in the world, yea & al sort of persons both old and young, would once leave their lascivious, wanton and unclene balades, & syng such godly and vertuous songes, as David teacheth them, wherby they might be avocated and called away from syn and excited and styred up unto vertue and goodnes. . . . Would God that al men of honor wold norish such Mynstrels in their houses, as David is, and that myght syng unto them bothe at dyner and supper, yea & at al other times these most swete & delectable songes of David so shold both they and al their family be disposed to lyve more vertuously, than many be now a daies, and be provoked to leave their pompeous, galant, wicked, venereal, fleshly, beastlyke and unclene maner of living. Wolde god also that al fathers and mothers, al masters and mastresses wold bryng up their children & servauntes in the singing of these most Godly songes. Again, wold God that al Scholemasters & teachers of youth, wold in stede of *Virgile, Ovide, Horas, Catullus, Tibullus, Propertius,* &c. teach these verses of David. For so shold they not only obtain eloquence, but also divine erudicion, godly knowledge, spiritual wisedom, & encrese in al kind of vertue, unto the great glory of God, the salvacion of their own soules, the right institucion of their own life, the great joye of theyr parentes, the good reporte of their teachers, and to the hie commodite of the Chrysten publyque weale. God graunte that it maye once thus come to passe.[22]

[22]Preface to *Davids Harpe ful of most delectable armony, newely stringed and set in tune by Thomas Becon* in *Works* (1564), Vol. I, sig. Dd2r-v. The *Harpe* was first published in 1542.

In addition to these principal motives, there was also the personal or private motive of Psalm versification in order to prepare the soul of the translator for death or to spend the time piously and profitably while in prison. An inspection of the list of metrical versions of the Psalms in the sixteenth century shows that not all of them were made by religious reformers or musicians, and that some of them apparently were intended solely for private reading, not for congregational singing. Henry Howard, Earl of Surrey, translated some Psalms during his final imprisonment. Sir Thomas Wyatt had translated the seven penitential Psalms as his last literary work, and in the same year Sir Thomas Smith, then a prisoner in the Tower, made the time pass by turning some of the Psalms into English verse.[23]

II

For the purpose of surveying the metrical Psalm translations of the sixteenth century in England it will be convenient to make a classification:

1. Early versions (1530-45) done under the influence of German versions
2. Experiments of the courtly makers
3. The Anglo-Genevan version (Sternhold and Hopkins)
4. Unsuccessful rivals of Sternhold and Hopkins
5. Versions done under the influence of Marot.

In the first class occur the *Goostly Psalmes* of Miles Coverdale, the great translator of the Bible. His book, which survives in a unique copy, consists of thirteen of the Psalms, two of them in two different versions, and a number of other spiritual songs, including a versified creed and ten commandments and translations of hymns. Coverdale was also the author of two versions of the Psalms in prose, one in 1535 in his Bible and the other his contribution to the Great Bible of 1539, which was later the version of the Psalms used in the Book of Common Prayer. Between 1535 and 1539 Coverdale became acquainted with the translation of Sebastian Münster and used it in his revisions for the Great Bible.

[23]Julian, *op. cit.*, p. 926. Julian is surely wrong in connecting Wyatt's Psalms with the Edwardian permission, as he seems to do on p. 916 b.

Since his verse translations show no trace of the influence of Münster, it is fair to infer that their composition belongs in the earlier period, around 1535. Coverdale was emancipated from the Vulgate by his knowledge of various German translations, and although he knew little Hebrew, he was able, by following the Germans, to approximate it more closely in some instances than if he had simply followed the Latin of the Vulgate.[24]

Coverdale used various verse forms: stanzas of four, seven, nine, ten, and thirteen lines, rhymed in various patterns. They are imitated from the German, and for most of them the German sources have been found. In translating Psalm 46 the Englishman used the meter of Luther's *"Ein' feste burg"* but translated the Psalm, not Luther's hymn based upon it. Coverdale's scansion is often bewildering:

> O Lorde, defende thou them therfore,
> And preserve us gracyously
> From this generacyon evermore,
> That persecute us so cruelly:
> For whan vanite and ydilnesse
> Is set by amonge men, doutless
> All are full of the ungodly.[25]

In the "Go little book" he repeats the wish, already quoted from his preface, that these songs may displace the "ballettes of filthiness" and then justifies himself educationally:

> Go lytle boke amonge mens chyldren
> And get the to theyr companye
> Teach them to synge the commaundementes ten
> And other ballettes of Gods glorye
> Be not ashamed I warande the
> Though thou be rude in songe and ryme
> Thou shalt to youth some occasion be
> In godly sportes to passe theyr tyme.[26]

Other representatives of this class of psalmists of the early period under the influence of German protestantism are Thomas Becon

[24]See Ernest Clapton, *Our Prayer Book Psalter* (London, S.P.C.K., 1934), which gives the two prose versions in parallel and the *Goostly Psalms* in an appendix.
[25]*Remains* (Parker Society), p. 568.
[26]*Ibid.*, p. 534.

and Robert Wisdom, who were forced to recant in 1543 and retired to the country to recant their recantation, and John Wedderburn the Scot, who had to flee to the Continent in 1539 and there absorbed the Lutheran atmosphere for four years before he returned home and compiled the volume known as the *Gude and Godlie Ballatis*, with spiritual parodies of profane songs and translations of German versions of the psalms.[27]

Sir Thomas Wyatt may be taken as representative of the courtly maker as psalmist. He brought to the task his interest in Italian poetry, his reflective moral strain so marked in the satires, and the vigorous, dramatic manner which often makes a sonnet translated by him from Petrarch into a new and original poem. Wyatt handled only the seven penitential Psalms, and he used as his source the prose version of them by Pietro Aretino.[28] For each Psalm there is a prologue, translated from Italian prose into English verse (eight-line stanzas rhyming *a b a b a b c c*); the prologue sets the psychological situation for the ensuing Psalm, and the whole series is supposed to derive from David's repentance for his sin in sending Uriah the Hittite into the forefront of the hottest battle so that he might have his wife Bathsheba. The Psalms are therefore romantic; they form a series of complaints, not so much for sin in general as for the traps and trammels of the flesh from a courtly point of view. David is made the author of a kind of *de remedia amoris*.

Wyatt translates the Psalms themselves in *terza rima*; the carry-over of the rhyme, and the poet's sense of the rhetorical possibilities of his pattern, give the verse a speed and energy which is individual. Miss Foxwell has pointed out that Wyatt often follows the

---

[27]Ed. A. F. Mitchell (Scottish Text Society, Vol. 39, 1897). Mitchell dates the volume as early as 1549, and Julian, considering it to be work done during Wedderburn's exile, places it between 1539 and 1543. A problem arises here because of the presence in *Gude and Godlie Ballatis* of a poem which appears in the 1549[?] edition of Hall's Proverbs of Solomon; another part of the poem is among those by Uncertain Authors in *Tottel's Miscellany*. See the letter by Hyder E. Rollins in the *Times* Literary Supplement, January 14, 1932. Professor Rollins attributes the poem, and another, to Hall on the strength of their appearance in the 1549[?] Proverbs under the title "Certayne Lessons." But because in 1550 the "Certayne Lessons" were dropped and a prose address to the reader substituted, I do not feel so confident of the attribution as Professor Rollins does.

[28]*The Poems of Sir Thomas Wiat*, ed. A. K. Foxwell (London, 1913), I, 202-250 and II, 129-41.

wording of the 1530 prose psalter, abandoning his Italian source for the greater directness and colloquial quality of the English. Even when he is following the English psalter, however, Wyatt makes the figures expand into dramatic and rhetorical situations:[29]

> To these Marmaydes and theyre baytes of error
>
> I stopp myn eris, with help of thy goodnes;
> And for I fele it comith alone of The,
> That to my hert thes foes have non acces
>
> I dare them bid; "Avoyd! Wreches and fle!
> "The Lord hath hard the voyce off my complaynt;
> Your engins take no more effect in me.
>
> The Lord hath herd I say and sen me faynt
> Under your hand, and piteth my distress;
> He shall do mak my sensis, by constraint,
>
> Obbey the rule that reson shall express,
> Wher the deceyte of yower glosing baite
> Made them usurp a powre in all exces.

That these "enemies" of which David speaks are appeals to the senses, "Marmaydes," rather than actual external enemies, will be a surprise to the ordinary reader of the 6th Psalm. But the translation is perfectly in keeping with the Petrarchan obsession, and the mind of the courtier has turned divine poetry to its own use.

Surrey wrote a sonnet in commendation of Wyatt's Psalms, and himself translated freely four Psalms from the Vulgate. They are in poulter's measure, with the exception of Psalm 55, which is in unrhymed hexameters. Padelford remarks that they "reflect the disillusionment of fortune that was so poignantly felt by sensitive and high-spirited men who were the victims of royal caprice." The work of Surrey's last imprisonment, they represent the courtier's only theme other than love: "the same tormenting sense of the treachery of friends, the malice of enemies and the mutability of things temporal."[30]

The version of the Psalms begun by Thomas Sternhold and com-

[29]*Ed. cit.*, I, 213-14.

[30]*The Poems of Henry Howard Earl of Surrey*, ed. F. M. Padelford (revised ed., Seattle, 1928), pp. 228-29.

pleted by John Hopkins and others after Sternhold's death in 1549 is, of course, the most famous of all the translations. Largely because it was the version adopted by the English exiles under Mary, it came to be venerated among the more zealous wing of the reformed church, and in Elizabethan times attained an almost official status. I am aware of no evidence for it, but a surmise might be made that the adoption (never official) of this version was a kind of sop to the Puritans. It is clear that they felt more attached to psalm-singing than did the more moderate Anglicans; and if some of their frenzy might be allayed by permitting them their own favorite version of the Psalms for singing, nothing would be lost in a doctrinal sense and much might be gained politically. Furthermore, there was no potential quarrel hidden in the Psalm version; such squabbles as had torn the church into factions at Frankfurt over the Edwardian prayer book might be avoided, because the Sternhold version was Edwardian in origin and yet acceptable to the most zealous of the exiles. It is clear that some reverence for Sternhold's own words appeared early, because the preface to the Psalms in *The forme of prayers. . . . Geneva . . 1556*, apologizes for altering in some places the verses "of hym whome for the gyftes that God had gevyn him we esteemed and reverenced";[31] the changes were made only to bring the text nearer to the sense of the Hebrew, and to include things which Sternhold had omitted.

Sternhold translated in all forty Psalms; his successor, John Hopkins, translated sixty. The other fifty were provided by various hands, the most interesting from a literary point of view being that of Thomas Norton, lawyer, translator, and dramatist, who furnished twenty-six Psalms. All of these men wrote in the 4.3.4.3 "ballad stanza" or Common Meter. Hopkins rhymed the four-beat lines as well as the three-beat lines, but Norton followed Sternhold in rhyming only the second and fourth lines. Some of the other contributors, such as Whittingham and Pullain and Kethe, tried to give variety of meter, and actually imitated the meters and used the tunes of the French version by Marot and Beza, but they were lost in the overwhelming number of Psalms in the Common Meter.

What happened, then, was the creation of a powerful and au-

[31] Sig. B4r.

thoritative mass of verse, heavily iambic in pattern and regular in stress, plain and bald in style. Sternhold even avoided the figurative language he found in his source, and tried by every means possible to make the content plain. He translates not only word, but idea. A well-known passage in the 34th[32] Psalm, for example, has had several conceits sifted out of it:

> The angel of the lorde doth pitche
> his tentes in every place.
> To save all suche as feare the Lord,
> that nothyng them deface.
> See and consider well therfore,
> that God is good and just.
>
> . . . .
> The mightie & the riche shall want
> yea thirst and hungre muche,
> But as for them that feare the lord,
> no lacke shalbe to suche.

The flatness and bathos of the conclusion should not obscure the point that "the young lions [who, in our King James Version] do lack and suffer hunger" have been translated to "the mighty and the rich," and the vividness of "O taste and see that the Lord is good" has been blunted into "see and consider well." (Whittingham, if he was the reviser, brought these images back into the text, presumably because they are in the Hebrew.)

The prolixity of much early Elizabethan verse, especially that written in fourteeners (and much of it was) may be a consequence of the Old Version of the Psalms. The translator trying to get the sense of the original was inclined to compress in the four-beat line and to pad in the three-beat line. In Sternhold's form of Common Meter, at any rate, the shorter lines are noticeably the weaker, and it is there, of course, that the translator is fumbling for his rhyme. But it would not be quite fair to say that from a literary point of view the influence of Sternhold and Hopkins was wholly pernicious. Their Psalms, commanding an audience roughly equivalent to the whole of the English-speaking race, constituted a body of verse that was plain, bare, regular in beat, iambic, strictly measured. It came at a time when English prosody was in confusion, and it

[32]The 33d in Sternhold's numbering. Sig. B7r.

offered some kind of order. Furthermore, since it continued in vogue through the whole latter half of the sixteenth century, it cannot be overlooked by the historian of Elizabethan poetry as a force working for that direct, plain, "mere English" quality against the lavish, ornamental, stylized manners which more than once threatened to dominate literary expression.

Several other metrical versions of the Psalms were produced around the middle of the century which can, in some sense, be considered unsuccessful rivals of the Sternhold-Hopkins translation. Of these the most interesting, both because of its authorship and because of its compromise character, is that by Matthew Parker, later Archbishop of Canterbury. According to his diary, it was done in 1557, but it was published only about ten years later, and then anonymously and without date. Parker's authorship, which is sometimes questioned (in *STC*, for example)[33] is proved by an acrostic signature in the metrical preface to Psalm 119.

In a long verse preface Parker justifies his effort by referring to the fathers of the church and to various scriptural texts; then he shows that he sympathizes with the old campaign of the reformers to replace secular songs with sacred Psalms:[34]

> The singyng man: and Poete must,
> with grave devine concurre:
> As Davids skill: all three discust,
> when he his harpe did sturre.
>
> Depart ye songes: lascivious,
> from lute, from harpe depart:
> Geve place to Psalmes: most vertuous,
> and solace there your harte.
>
> Ye songes so nice: ye sonnets all,
> of lothly lovers layes:
> Ye worke mens myndes: but bitter gall,
> by phansies pevishe playes.

He first intended his version, he says, for his private solace only, but was persuaded to publish:

[33]*STC* 2729.
[34]Sig. A3r-B4r.

And where at first: I secret ment,
but them my selfe to sing:
Yet frendes requestes: made me relent,
thus them abrode to bring.

Parker stands curiously in a middle position between the Puritans and the courtiers. His verse forms show a predominance of Common Meter, rhymed in the manner of Hopkins. And his diction and style resemble the plain manner of the Old Version. But in some of his versions Parker uses very elaborate schemes: Psalm 102 is in four-line stanzas of four feet each, with every stanza linked by rhyme to the stanza preceding it and the stanza following. Psalm 101 is translated in stanzas of four lines, of which the first three are four-foot lines and the last a two-foot line. This gives an effect somewhat similar to that of Wyatt's ballets, with the short line acting as a kind of chorus or refrain. Psalm 86 is done in six-line stanzas with a refrain, the line-ends rhyming *a b a b c c* and the hemistichs rhyming in couplets. A note in the margin calls attention to the fact that "These ceasures [hemistichs] have perfect sence red, severally or jointly."

As published, the Psalms of Parker were provided with tunes by the great Thomas Tallis, of the Chapel Royal, and a versified description of the tunes gave the general emotional character of each. The tunes were considered to be common within limits; that is, the reader was urged to choose a tune suitable to the character of the Psalm. A concession to Protestant individualism, however, shows itself in a license for freedom of selection: "For what Psalme or songe, one mans spirite shall judge grave and sad, some other shall thinke it pleasaunt. And what one mans eare shall thinke pleasaunt, another shall judge it sower and severe. And therefore in this diversitie I leave it to every mans spirite as God shall move hym: and to every mans eare, as nature shall frame hym."[35]

Parker's Psalms apparently had very little influence; so few copies of the one edition printed have survived that it has been suggested that the edition was never published but used for private presentation only. The literary interest of this version arises from its compromise between the courtly manner and the style of the Puritans.

[35]Sig. VV2v-VV3r.

Other translators, such as the Puritan printer and preacher Robert Crowley, and his associates and friends, Lady Elizabeth Fane and Francis Seager, translated the Psalms, or a selection from them, into verse for singing. John Hall and William Hunnis translated Psalms and Proverbs, and even William Forrest, the Catholic, who became a chaplain to Queen Mary, left a metrical translation of the Psalms in manuscript. The vogue was not limited, in the middle years of the century, to any religious group or to any literary school or to any level of poetical talent.

In France the Psalms had appealed to genius as well as to piety; Clément Marot was as much the artist in his versions as in his epigrams or epistles or complaints. Genius responded in England, too, but the English version remained an art work and nothing more, circulating in manuscript and remaining unpublished until the nineteenth century. It is the work of Sir Philip Sidney and his sister, Mary, Countess of Pembroke.[36] At the opposite extreme from the version of Sternhold and Hopkins, it is dependent upon the French version of Marot and Beza, and when it departs from the French models it does so in order to attempt more elaborate and subtle exercises in versification than even the French poet attempted.

Sidney made it clear in his *Apologie for Poetrie* that he was aware of the essential poetic nature of the Psalms:

And may I not presume a little further, to shew the reasonableness of this word *Vates?* And say that the holy Davids Psalmes are a divine Poem? If I doo, I shall not do it without the testimonie of great learned men, both auncient and moderne. But even the name Psalmes will speake for mee, which, being interpreted, is nothing but songes: then that it is fully written in meeter, as all learned Hebricians agree, although the rules be not yet fully found: lastly and principally, his handeling his prophecy, which is meerely poetical. For what els is the awaking his musicall instruments; the often and free changing of persons; his notable Prosopopeias, when he maketh you as it were, see God comming in his Majestie; his telling of the Beastes joyfulnes, and hills leaping, but a heavenlie poesie, wherein almost hee sheweth himselfe a passionate lover of that unspeakable and everlasting beautie to be seene by the eyes of the minde, only cleered by fayth?[37]

[36]*Works*, ed. A. Feuillerat (Cambridge, 1923), Vol. III.
[37]*Apologie for Poetrie*, ed. E. S. Shuckburgh (Cambridge, 1891), pp. 6-7.

What more natural, then, than to turn the Psalms into English verse, and show that the language he had defended in his *Apologie* was as fit for the expression of divine poetry as French was? Of the forty-three Psalms which Sidney completed himself, fourteen are composed in direct imitation of the meter of a Psalm in the Marot-Beza version.[38] Still others adopt a rhyme-scheme from the French and vary the meter. But the general debt to the French original is greater still. Sidney shared Marot's ambition of illustrating in the Psalms a wide variety of meters, making the verse correspond with the atmosphere or feeling of the particular Psalm. And in doing this, Sidney compiled what might be regarded as a School of English Versification. Accentual hexameters are illustrated in Psalm 17, in a kind of epic stanza of seven lines, chosen apparently to carry the weight of the cosmic upheavals described in that Psalm; again in Psalm 15, we find a thirteen-line poem in hexameters, all on the same rhyme. In Psalm 13 he uses a measure which reminds the modern reader of Herrick: iambic pentameter lines rhyming in couplets but separated by short lines (one foot with feminine ending) also rhyming in couplets. There are many varieties of six-line stanza, the modes of rhyming suggesting the variety in the sestets of Sidney's sonnets, and the combination of lines of various length showing the most careful and subtle ear for effects. When he uses anything as simple as the ballad stanza of Hopkins (as in Psalm 24) he makes lines 1 and 3 hexameters with a feminine ending, and lines 2 and 4 tetrameter and masculine. Successive Psalms which do not derive directly from the French show what the process was: to alter and experiment with various combinations of line length, rhyme scheme, and type of foot, varying more than·

[38]Since this can be easily verified, it is difficult to understand the statement in Malcolm W. Wallace, *The Life of Sir Philip Sidney* (Cambridge, 1915), p. 325: "His intimacy with many of the greatest contemporary men of letters in France suggests the possibility of his indebtedness to the version of Marot and Beza, but there is no similarity either in the form of stanzas or in phraseology." There is no correction of this statement, as there is no serious criticism of the Sidney Psalms, in Mona Wilson, *Sir Philip Sidney* (1931); E. M. Denkinger, *Immortal Sidney* (1932); K. O. Myrick, *Sir Philip Sidney as a Literary Craftsman* (1935); or C. H. Warren, *Sir Philip Sidney* (1936). Professor Pratt, in chapter xi of *The Music of the French Psalter of 1562*, notes meters from the French which Sidney used, but the musicologist does not of course concern himself with the rhyme schemes.

one element at a time so that the process does not look academic but illustrates a marvelous variety and ingenuity. Psalms 28 and 29, for example, are both in tetrameter, but the former is a five-line stanza in trochaic and the latter a three-line stanza in iambic. Psalms 25, 26, and 27 form a little series of exercises in the six-line stanza, with experimentation in line length: first, lines 1-4 trimeter and the other two tetrameter, then lines 1, 2, 4 and 5 trimeter and 3 and 6 pentameter; finally, lines 1-4 tetrameter and the last two dimeter. At the same time he shifts the rhyme scheme around, from *ababcc* to *aabccb* and then back to his first scheme.

It is remarkable that all this virtuosity does not give a stilted effect. The Psalms have been praised, notably by Donne, who apparently saw that these versions are comparable with Marot's and wished they might replace Sternhold and Hopkins in the church:

> The songs are these, which heavens high holy Muse
> Whisper'd to *David*, *David* to the Jewes:
> And *Davids* Successors, in holy zeale,
> In formes of joy and art do re-reveale
> To us so sweetly and sincerely too,
> That I must not rejoyce as I would doe
> When I behold that these Psalmes are become
> So well attyr'd abroad, so ill at home,
> So well in Chambers, in thy Church so ill,
> As I can scarce call that reform'd untill
> This be reform'd; Would a whole State present
> A lesser gift than some one man hath sent?
> And shall our Church, unto our Spouse and King
> More hoarse, more harsh than any other, sing?[39]

Ruskin praised the Sidney Psalms for their directness, and he proposed to make them one of the textbooks in his St. George's schools, publishing a selection of them for that purpose under the title *Rock Honeycomb*.[40] But the writers on Sidney have paid little attention to the Psalms, and most critics who have read them have started with the phrases of the King James Version in their ears and of course have found Sidney unbearable.

These five versions, Coverdale's, Wyatt's, the Sternhold-Hop-

[39]*Poetical Works*, ed. H. J. C. Grierson (Oxford, 1912), I, 349.
[40]*The Works of Ruskin*, ed. E. T. Cook and A. Wedderburn (1907), Vol. XXXI.

kins, the Parker, and the Sidney, merely represent five sixteenth-century approaches to a task. There were many Psalm translators in the period, of course, whose motive is not so clear and whose achievement is not so significant for the historian of poetry. What we are trying to understand is the variety of ways in which a particular problem was solved by writers of verse in the English Renaissance. A study of the metrical versions of the Psalms is useful for that purpose because the Psalms immediately involve the question of the relationship between the divine and the secular, because no translator can attempt to put the Psalms into English verse without showing, perhaps more clearly than elsewhere, his conceptions of the function and purpose of poetry, and because the versified Psalms as represented in their various versions in the sixteenth century reveal all levels of literary appeal, from the most vulgar and general to the most limited and esoteric.

It has been suggested that the Sternhold-Hopkins version had an important influence in strengthening the iambic tendency in English verse and in establishing a kind of norm for plain diction in verse; Sidney's version has been interpreted as an Art of English Verse. Between these two lies the whole story of the development of the art of poetry to its height in the late sixteenth and early seventeenth centuries. That development can only be traced clearly by an examination of those fundamental subjects and themes which moved to expression the spirits of men. When the history of Elizabethan poetry comes to be written, it will be not so much a series of biographical sketches, with critical remarks thrown in from any random point of view, as a study and interpretation of the great commonplaces, with accurate description of the variety of ways in which the treatment of them became art. One of these great commonplaces was the Book of Psalms.

Dryden's *Georgics* and English Predecessors

By Helene Maxwell Hooker

I

THE problem here dealt with is Dryden's method of translation. Specifically, Dryden's translation of Virgil's *Georgics* has been examined in order to throw light on his indebtedness to his English predecessors and on the manner in which he made use of them.

There is almost no scholarship to assist in such a study. The German dissertations on the Virgil translations are worthless. A few English and American scholars have dealt very briefly with the problem, generally concerning themselves with only one poet, and always going astray because they failed to recognize that the seventeenth-century Virgil translations represent a continuous chain of, development in which it is impossible to evaluate the work of any one man without knowing all of the others.[1]

The most valuable contribution to this subject is Mr. J. McG. Bottkol's recent article, "Dryden's Latin Scholarship."[2] Mr. Bottkol's method has been to concentrate on the effect which Latin texts and commentaries available to Dryden produced in his translations. This method is impractical until the spadework of examining in detail all previous English translations has been carried out. Mr.

---

[1] For German scholarship see: K. F. J. Nick, *De Virgilii carminibus a Drydena poeta in linguam Britannicam translatis* (Jena, 1868); J. Diekmann, *Dryden's Virgil Compared with the Latin Original* (Rostock, 1874); Charles Macpherson, *Über die Vergil-Ubersetzung des John Dryden* (Berlin, 1910). English and American scholarship includes: John Conington, "The English Translators of Virgil" in *Miscellaneous Writings* (London, 1872), I, 137-97. Pp. 146-59 includes a partial chronological description of the seventeenth-century translators. The discussion of borrowing is slight and unsatisfactory. *The Poetical Works of John Dryden*, ed. G. R. Noyes (1908), pp. 1000-1, discusses one case of borrowing in Book III; Mark Van Doren, *The Poetry of John Dryden* (1931), p. 106, speaks in a general way of Dryden's borrowings from Lauderdale, but does not mention other sources; Allen Griffith Chester, *Thomas May: Man of Letters, 1595-1650* (Philadelphia, 1932), speaks very briefly of Dryden's use of May, but gives no detail; Douglas Bush, *Mythology and the Romantic Tradition in English Poetry* (Cambridge, Mass., 1937) does not pretend to discuss the problem; however, on p. 16 there are a few remarks about Dryden's borrowings in the *Æneis*.

[2] *Modern Philology*, XL (1942-43), 241-54.

Bottkol has not made allowances for the extensive part which they played in Dryden's work. He suggests that Dryden

> sat with a favorite edition open before him (Prateus, Ruaeus, Casaubon, or Cnipping), read the original carefully, often the Latin prose *Interpretatio*, and invariably studied the accompanying annotations. When he came to a difficult or disputed passage, he repeatedly turned to other editors, studied and compared their varying opinions, and then chose to follow one authority or another or even to make a new interpretation for himself. Also he had open before him on the table one or more earlier English translations, particularly those which were written in heroic couplets. From these he often took rhymes, stray phrases, even whole lines and passages.[3]

Mr. Bottkol's picture, though fundamentally true, must be amplified. We know now that in addition to the Latin editors open before him, Dryden used considerably more than one or two English translations in the preparation of the *Georgics*. The number is no less than nine.

Dryden's indebtedness to his predecessors surpasses anything that has been hinted at previously. Aware of the dangers of the parallel-passage method of estimating borrowings or indebtedness, I have proceeded by the most cautious and conservative method. I have taken no account of vague general resemblances or of similarities or even identities of wording and phrasing within the line.[4] Neither have I taken account of identical rhymes or phrases in two or more translators unless they are used to render the same passage in the original. What I have considered have been identical couplets, identical rhyme words, or identical lines when two or more translators used them in rendering the same passage in Virgil. Such identities, especially when they occur by the hundred, can by no stretch of the imagination be considered accidental.

Dryden's version is the culmination of the genealogical succession of the seventeenth-century translations of Virgil. The great ancestor is Thomas May, whose *Virgil's Georgicks Englished* was published in 1628. Among his descendants are John Ogilby; Abraham Cowley; Richard Maitland, Earl of Lauderdale; Knightly

---

[3]*Ibid.*, p. 243.

[4]Cf. Dryden, II, 350: "These rules consider'd well, with early care," and May, II, 284: "These things consider'd well, remember thou."

Chetwood; John Sheffield, Earl of Mulgrave, Marquis of Normanby, and Duke of Buckinghamshire; Sir Charles Sedley; Joseph Addison; Henry Sacheverell; the anonymous translator of *"Amor semper idem"* in *Sylvae;* and, greatest of all, John Dryden. Each translator, while making his own contribution, borrowed something from previous translators. This habit of appropriation and adaptation was so widespread that it cannot be lightly dismissed as plagiarism. It became the traditional and accepted method of Virgil translation. Dryden made use of the tradition, and displayed his genius by weaving borrowed pieces and original passages into a single, superb fabric.[5]

[5]Translations of the *Georgics* examined for this paper are listed below. They are listed *en bloc* because as such they comprise a bibliography of English translations of the poem through the publication of Lauderdale's version. As such it corrects several errors. The items marked with an asterisk were not, so far as the writer has been able to determine, used by Dryden:

*A[braham] F[leming], *The Bucoliks of Publius Virgilius Maro . . . Together with his Georgiks . . . Conteyning foure bookes* (1589)

*[John Brinsley], *Virgils Eclogues, With His Booke De Apibus* (1620; 1633)

Tho[mas] May, *Virgil's Georgicks Englished* (1628)

Abraham Cowley, "A Translation out of Virgil," in the essay "Of Agriculture"

*Richard Crashaw, "Out of Virgil, in Praise of Spring" in *Delights of the Muses* (1646). [A translation of Book II, ll. 323-45]

*Henry Vaughn, in *The Mount of Olives* (1652) [A translation of part of the Fourth Georgic]

John Ogilby, *The Works of Publius Virgilius Maro* (1649; 1650; 1654)

[John Sheffield], E[arl] of M[ulgrave], "Part of Virgil's IV. Georgick" in Dryden's *Miscellany Poems*, Part I (1684), pp. 169-72.

[Knightly] Chetwood, "The Praises of Italy out of Virgil's Second Georgic," in Dryden's *Miscellany Poems*, Part I (1684), pp. 310-13.

[Richard Maitland, Earl of Lauderdale], "Part of Virgils 4th Georgick," in Dryden's *Miscellany Poems*, Part II (1685), pp. 145-54; "The First Book of Virgil's Georgicks. Translated into English Verse by the Right Honourable John Earl of Lauderdale" in *Miscellany Poems*, Part IV (1694), pp. 217-53; *The Works of Virgil* [1718]

"*Amor omnibus idem:* Or, the Force of Love in all Creatures," in Dryden's *Miscellany Poems*, Part III (1693), pp. 335-42

H[enry] Sacheverill, "From Virgil's 1st Georgick," in Dryden's *Miscellany Poems*, Part III (1693), pp. 413-17

Jo[seph] Addison, "A Translation of all Virgil's 4th Georgick, except the Story of Aristeus" in Dryden's *Miscellany Poems*, Part IV, (1694), pp. 58-86

John Dryden, *The Works of Virgil* (1697)

Sir Charles Sedley, "The Fourth Book of Virgil," in *The Miscellaneous Works*, ed. Capt. [William] Ayloffe (1702) [date of composition unknown] pp. 174-213

II

To illustrate the complexities of the problem and to demonstrate the caution that must be exercised in tracing Dryden's borrowings, let us examine two specific passages. The first must be taken in connection with the editorial comment that accompanied it.

In 1724, when William Benson published his examination of Dryden's first book of the *Georgics*, his attitude was one of complete disparagement. Many of the lines were very badly rendered. As an illustration of Dryden's failure to measure up to the requirements of acceptable Virgilian translation, he gloomily cited (among many others) lines 304-5:

> Sow beans and clover in a rotten soil,
> And millet rising from your annual toil;[6]

"These two mean lines," he disapprovingly pointed out, "are taken almost entirely from Mr May, only that Mr Dryden has omitted the proper word, *vere*, which Mr May does not."[7] The lines by May to which Benson referred read:

> Sow beans i' th' spring, clave grass in rotten soil,
> And willet, that requires a yearly toil,[8]

At first glance the resemblance between the two versions seems beyond all question. However, we are brought up short when we turn to the translation made by Dryden's friend, Richard Maitland, Earl of Lauderdale, and find:

> Sow beans and cinque-foil in a mellow soil,
> And millet springing from your annual toil;[9]

Comparison of the three versions shows immediately that Benson was wrong in describing May as the source for the lines in question. In this couplet Dryden mainly derived from Lauderdale, even to the almost verbatim use of line 215. But we must also note that Lauderdale derived from May, and that in the three versions we find a striking similarity, with identical rhyme words.

[6]In quotations, spelling and punctuation are modernized.
[7]*Virgil's Husbandry, or An Essay on the Georgics*. . . . (1724).
[8]*Virgil's Georgicks Englished* (1628), ll. 233-34.
[9]Ll. 214-15.

For one more illustration of this fundamental point, let us examine a longer passage—lines 383-98 in Book VI on the restoration to health and activity of ailing bees. Dryden's version begins (ll. 383-86):

> This when thou seest, Galbanean odours use,
> And honey in the sickly hive infuse,
> Thro reeden pipes convey the golden flood,
> T'invite the people to their wonted food.

In his earlier translation of this same passage Thomas May wrote (ll. 305-8):

> For this of gums a fumigation use,
> And into th'hive in pipes of reed infuse
> Honey, t'invite them to a well-known food;
> With these the taste of beaten galt is good;

The close correspondence in May's and Dryden's rhyme schemes is obvious. Continuing with the next couplet we read in Dryden (ll. 387-88):

> Mix it with thicken'd juice of sodden wines,
> And raisins from the grapes of Psythian vines:

Comparing these lines with those of his fellow translators, we find that here, too, there was a well-established precedent. Thomas May set the fashion when he wrote (ll. 309-10):

> Dried roses too, and thick decocted wine,
> And loose hung clusters from the Psythian vine,

Nearly a quarter of a century later the despised John Ogilby varied this slightly with (ll. 302-3):

> To these Cecropian thyme and cent'ry join,
> And grapes which dangle on the *Psythian* vine.

Lauderdale chose to follow May's rhyme pattern, writing (ll. 307-8):

> If with all these you mingle well-burnt wine,
> Or sun-dried raisins from the *Psythian* vine.

Addison closes the procession with (l. 359): "And raisins ripen'd on the *Psythian* vine." Here we have a good example of the genealogical descent, with May, Ogilby, Lauderdale, and Addison all following the same close trend—a direction which Dryden found acceptable.

Continuing with the next line, Dryden gives us (l. 390): "And, with Cecropian thyme, strong-scented centaury." Although Dryden does not use Ogilby's rhyme word, his translation of line 302 (see the Ogilby couplet cited immediately above) leaves no doubt of the descent.[10]

Progressing to the next couplet, we find in Dryden (ll. 391-92):

> A flow'r there is that grows in meadow ground,
> *Amellus* call'd, and easy to be found;

Here again there is precedent. Ogilby wrote (ll. 304-5):

> There is a flower which grows in meadow ground,
> Swains call it *Amello*, easy to be found,

Joseph Addison followed this lead with (ll. 360-61):

> Besides there grows a flow'r in marshy ground
> Its name *Amellus*, easy to be found;

The next couplet (ll. 392-93) does not suggest any of Dryden's predecessors. Proceeding with lines 394-96, Dryden gives us:

> A wood of leaves and vi'let-purple boughs:
> The flow'r itself is glorious to behold,
> And shines on altars like refulgent gold:

The descent of these lines is easily traceable to Thomas May, who wrote (ll. 314-16):

> For from one root he spreads a wood of boughs.
> Whose many leaves, although the flower be gold,
> Black violets dim purple color hold.

Dryden's concluding couplet reads (ll. 397-98):

> Sharp to the taste, by shepherds near the stream
> Of *Mella* found, and hence they gave the name.

---

[10]Sir Charles Sedley's version reads "Clusters of raisins, thyme, and centaury" (l. 300), which corresponds very nearly with Dryden's line. Although it is tempting and convenient to argue for Sedley's priority to Dryden, the question is still unsettled. See below, pp. 306-8.

His lines derive from Ogilby's, which read (ll. 310-11):

> Sharp in the taste; wise shepherds gather them
> In flow'ry vales, near *Mella's* sacred stream;

These two brief illustrations of Dryden's method can be multiplied many times.[11] Comparing his translations of the *Georgics* with those of his predecessors, we find that while he used the Latin commentaries freely, he relied heavily on his fellow translators for telling phrases and rhymes. To some of his debtors he was explicitly grateful. On one occasion, when he drew on the Earl of Mulgrave, he was almost assertively willing to show where he had got his material. In more plebeian cases he maintained a complete silence, and it is only through a line-by-line comparison of the texts that we can establish the relationship.[12]

Dryden's borrowings fall into the following classifications:
  (1) Use of an end word or phrase in order to give the rhyme for a couplet, as in IV, 173-74:

> And deck with fruitful trees the fields around,
> And with refreshing waters deck the ground.

Compare May, IV, 137-38:

> Wearing his hands with labour hard, and round
> Bestow a friendly watering on the ground.

  (2) The almost verbatim use of a line or couplet as in I, 344-45:

> From hence uncertain seasons we may know;
> And when to reap the grain, and when to sow;

Compare Lauderdale, I, 252-53:

> From hence we may uncertain seasons know,
> Both when to reap the grain, and when to sow;

---

[11]A few examples from Book I: Dryden, 38-39 / Lauderdale, 27-28; Dryden, 179-80 / Lauderdale, 116-17; Dryden, 195 / Lauderdale, 124; Dryden, 208-10 / Lauderdale, 135 / May, 141-42 / Ogilby, 147-48; Dryden, 254-55 / Ogilby, 184 / Lauderdale, 171-72; Dryden, 265 / May, 185; Dryden, 268-69 / Ogilby, 195-96; Dryden, 270-71 / Lauderdale, 183-84.

[12]For a line-by-line study of these borrowings, see my forthcoming edition of Dryden's *Georgics.*

(3) A combination of lines, the first from one translator, the second from another, to make a couplet, as in III, 72-73:

> With which inspir'd, I brook no dull delay:
> *Cytheron* loudly calls me to my way;

Compare Lauderdale, III, 54: "With mighty things proceed; hence all delay," and Ogilby, III, 48: "*Cithæron* calls aloud, ah, come away."

(4) A combination of couplets, as in III, 747-50:

> The victor horse, forgetful of his food,
> The palm renounces, and abhors the flood.
> He paws the ground, and on his hanging ears,
> A doubtful sweat in clammy drops appears:

Compare Ogilby, III, 533-34:

> The conquering steed, mindless of war, or food,
> Unhappy falls, and leaves the cooling flood,

and May, III, 451-52:

> Oft with his hoofs he beats the earth, his ears
> Hang down, his sweat uncertainly appears:

(5) A combination of phrases from two translators in order to form a line, as in III, 19: "Of *Parian* stone a temple will I raise." Compare May, III, 16: "A marble temple in the field I'll raise," and Lauderdale, III, 18-19:

> Of conquer'd *Greece*, a temple shall arise
> Of *Parian* stone, . . .[18]

(6) Use of a French or Latin commentary for interpretation, but of an English translation for rhyme. William Benson pointed out an example of this procedure in II, 130-31:

> The Thracian vines in richer soils abound,
> The Mareotique grow in barren ground,

"Pontanus having made this mistake," he observed, "Ruaeus follows him, and Mr Dryden, Ruaeus; and in this passage he shows an implicit submission to the Reverend Father; for these lines are Mr

---

[18]The original (*vide* Virgil, III, 13) does not mention the type of stone.

May's, only he has altered them to Ruaeus' interpretation, as the reader will perceive by Mr May's verses [ll. 99-100].

> The Thracian vines in barren soils abound,
> The Mareotic thrive in richer ground."[14]

These examples show us that all discussions of borrowings or indebtedness on Dryden's part must be accompanied by utmost circumspection in judgment until all the evidence is at hand.

III

Let us now examine the specific men of letters to whom Dryden was beholden. He himself tells us that his friend Gilbert Dolben presented him with copies of "all the several editions of Virgil, and all the commentaries of those editions in Latin."[15] This statement implies that Dryden relied on the Latin editions. But, as we have already seen, the Latin commentaries were supplemented by good hard use of the English rhymed translations, almost all of which were subjected to his critical scrutiny.

These translations were to be found in three places: (1) the two printed versions of the entire *Georgics*, notably by Thomas May and John Ogilby; (2) the manuscript translation of the entire poem, made by the Earl of Lauderdale; and (3) portions printed either in the Miscellanies edited by Dryden or in other places. Each contributor deserves our attention for the part he played in Dryden's work.

Thomas May

One of Dryden's most extensive silent partners was the poet, historian, and Parliamentarian, Thomas May (1595-1650), whose English translation appeared in 1628.[16] Today May is but little known, and his literary work almost entirely overlooked. During

---

[14] *Virgil's Husbandry* (1724), [H2v]—[H]3. The present study does not attempt to discuss this aspect of Dryden's translation.

[15] "Postscript to the Reader."

[16] *Virgil's Georgicks Englished.* Two editions, with identical title pages, were published. The first is generally accessible. Only three copies of the second are known to exist. They are in the Bodleian, Newberry, and Huntington libraries.

his lifetime, however, he was far from being the complete cipher he now seems. He was a man of many activities. If he is remembered it is as an active politician, prominent in the Parliamentary party (and therefore posthumously disgraced). But he also found time to be a man of letters. His literary friends included Ben Jonson, Endymion Porter, Thomas Carew, Sir Kenelm Digby, Sir Richard Fanshawe, Sir John Suckling, and Sir Aston Cokaine.[17] William Benson described him as, "A rival to Sir William Davenant for the bays, but unsuccessful in his pretension. He writ several plays, and translated Lucan, and Virgil's Georgics."[18]

As the ancestor of the seventeenth-century translations of the *Georgics*, May's nearly forgotten version assumes distinct importance. Compared with the versions of later translators, May's couplets often seem to be characterized by metrical roughness and a marked terseness of expression. For us, however, its primary interest lies not in an evaluation of its literary merits, but in the fact that this early venture in Virgil served as a crutch and a guide for subsequent translators. Ogilby, Lauderdale, Addison, Sedley, and Dryden are among the company who utilized May without acknowledgment.

Describing May's *Georgics*, Benson stated, "This last, which is but a very moderate performance, Mr Dryden had always before his eyes, and through haste, I suppose, very frequently took two, or three lines, even sometimes five, or six, almost together, out of this obscure author. There are in this Georgic [II], I believe, almost a hundred of Mr May's lines, very little altered, and in the four Georgics, I believe there may be found more than as many hundred, if any body has leisure enough to make such a search."[19]

As has already been pointed out, Benson—either through ignorance or oversight—did not distinguish between Dryden's borrow-

[17]There is surprisingly little material on May. Professor Chester's study, *supra*, p. 273, is the only recent work. There is a good article in *Biographia Britannica*, Vol. V, and the *Dict. Nat. Biog.* also contains information. Among contemporary references to him see Ben Jonson, "To my chosen friend, the learned translator of Lucan, Thomas May, Esq."; Sir John Suckling, "A session of the poets"; Thomas Heywood, "Hierarchie of blessed angels"; Sir Aston Cokaine, *Small poems of divers sorts* (1658), 134.

[18]*Virgil's Husbandry*, Sig. [H1v]-H2
[19]*Ibid.*, Sig. [H1v]-H2

ings from May and from Lauderdale. Therefore his case is somewhat overstated. Benson's own quotation is an illustration of what is often the case: rhymes that seem to derive from May actually come into Dryden's pages through Lauderdale— a debt that Dryden freely acknowledged. However, the reverse of the picture is also true: rhymes that at first glance seem to come from Lauderdale we sometimes find, by the clue of a word or phrase peculiar to May but not present in Lauderdale, have come from *Virgil's Georgicks Englished*. Although Dryden affirmed his indebtedness to Lauderdale and not once mentioned Thomas May, the amount of his borrowing from the two men is about equal.[20] In fact, it was to their translations that Dryden turned most often when he needed help in the facilitation of his great undertaking.

Dryden's borrowings from May are of many kinds, ranging from the mere borrowing of end words to the appropriation of entire lines. Sometimes, as in the following passage, it is clear that as Dryden wrote, May's *Georgicks* lay close at hand, and that they were very useful not only in furnishing rhyme words, but also in providing the approach: Dryden, I, 320-33:

> For this, thro' twelve bright signs Apollo guides
> The year, and earth in sev'ral climes divides.
> Five girdles bind the skies, the torrid zone
> Glows with the passing and repassing sun.

May, I, 238-41:

> And therefore through twelve signs bright Phoebus guides
> The world, and th'earth in several climes divides.
> Five zones divide the heavens, the torrid one
> Still red, still heated by the burning sun.[21]

---

[20]See below.

[21]A few more examples of this practice, ranging from two lines to six and all taken from Book II, include: Dryden, 162-63 / May, 129-30; Dryden, 348-49 / May, 282-83; Dryden, 360-65 / May, 294-99; Dryden, 438-43 / May, 355-60. It cannot be sufficiently emphasized that these illustrations are highly selective, and that there are many more. The mere listing of line numbers, however, does not afford proof, and there is not room for prolonged quotation in an article of this length.

Occasionally he appropriates a line almost verbatim, altering it only very slightly. In the second line of the following couplet (the first line of which is also found useful) such a method is followed: Dryden, II, 247-48:

> The nature of their sev'ral soils now see,
> Their strength, their colour, their fertility:

May, II, 195-96:

> Now all soils several natures let us see
> Their strengths, their colours, and fertility:[22]

Sometimes, but not often, Dryden uses a line exactly as it appears in May, a practice illustrated in the first line of the following couplet: Dryden, II, 272-73:

> Then seek Tarentum's lawns, and farthest coast,
> On such a field as hapless Mantua lost:

May, II, 216-17:

> Then seek Tarentum's lawns, and farthest coast,
> Such fields as hapless Mantua has lost,[23]

Occasionally Dryden uses May's rhyme word (if it is a verb) while changing the tense, as in Dryden, II, 323-24:

> Salt earth and bitter are not fit to sow,
> Nor will be tam'd or mended with the plough.

May, II, 258-59:

> The earth that's salt, or bitter, bad for sowing,
> (For they will never be made good by plowing.)

[22]Other examples, all taken from Book III, include: Dryden, 372 / May, 289; Dryden, 451 / May, 312; Dryden, 806 / May, 600.

[23]This couplet is only one of the many examples of the frequent dependence on May's rhyme schemes by subsequent Virgil translators. Ogilby, II, 215-16, reads:
> "Seek pleasant groves, and rich Tarentum's coast,
> And plains which woeful Mantua hath lost."
Lauderdale, II, reads:
> "Choose distant fields on the Tarentine coast;
> Such fertile plains unhappy Mantua lost;"
Other examples of Dryden's verbatim use of May are: I, Dryden, 210 / May, 142; III, Dryden, 372 / May, 289; Dryden, 452 / May, 313 (in this case Dryden uses May in preference to Lauderdale); Dryden, 806 / May, 600; Dryden, 736 / May, 538.

But Dryden's most frequent use of May is to take his rhyme word, translating the remainder of the line as he chooses. For example, see Dryden, II, 299: "Well cloth'd with cheerful grass, and ever green," and May, II, 240: "Which cloaths herself in her own grassy green."[24] Sometimes he uses May alone. Sometimes he combines a line based on May with a line based on Lauderdale or Ogilby, to produce a couplet or a triplet. Thus, we find that Dryden, I, 422-44:

> What cares must then attend the toiling swain;
> Or when the low'ring spring, with lavish rain,
> Beats down the slender stem and bearded grain,

has distinct echoes in the following lines: Lauderdale, I, 318: "Or shall I here instruct the lab'ring swain"; May, I, 336: "Or when the showery spring doth promise rain?" and Ogilby, I, 356: "Or when green stalks but swell with milky grain?"[25]

These illustrations afford ample proof of the fact that although Dryden never mentioned May or his translation, he was thoroughly familiar with his version of the *Georgics*. In a brief reference to these borrowings Professor Alan Chester writes, "It is a compliment to the older poet, perhaps, that Dryden did not disdain to purloin more than a hundred lines from May's translation of the Georgics . . ."[26]

My figures suggest that Professor Chester's estimate requires a fundamental revision that should be applied in two directions. In the first place, if by "purloining" is meant the appropriation of identical or nearly identical lines, the number used by Dryden is considerably less than the number indicated. The sum total of identical lines taken from May is six—one in Georgic I, three in Georgic II, two in Georgic III, and none in Georgic IV. There are

---

[24]Examples of this type of borrowing are too numerous to mention more than most briefly. A few examples, taken at random, are: II, Dryden, 17-18 / May, 15-17; Dryden, 37-38 / May, 33-34; Dryden, 43-44 / May, 39-40; Dryden, 256-57 / May, 203-4; Dryden, 265 / May, 208; Dryden, 356-57/ May, 290-91; Dryden, 403-4 / May, 324-25; Dryden, 531-32 / May, 423-24.

[25]Other examples of this method are: III, Dryden, 171-72 / May, 128-29 / Lauderdale, 156; Dryden, 356-59 / "Anon." in *Examen Poeticum*, 31 / May, 276, 278-79; Dryden, 446-49 / Ogilby, 308 / Lauderdale, 334 / "Anon." in *Examen Poeticum*, 110-11.

[26]*Op. cit.*, p. 152.

eight lines that are nearly identical—five in Georgic III and three in Georgic IV. If, however, Professor Chester has in mind the use of rhyme words, his calculations must be expanded and revised upward to a little more than twice his estimated figure. For Dryden used at least 230 of May's rhyme words. They distribute themselves in the following order: Georgic I, seventeen; Georgic II, one hundred and four; Georgic III, fifty-eight, and Georgic IV, fifty-one. In addition, scattered throughout the four books are forty-seven lines whose sources are questionable. That is, they might with equal ease come from May, Ogilby, or Lauderdale. From these figures it is perfectly clear that as an aid to translation, Thomas May was distinctly useful.

John Ogilby

Another silent partner was John Ogilby (1600-1676), whose translation of Virgil was published first in 1649, again in 1650, and in 1654 reissued in a revised, sumptuous edition. Although he got some financial profit from the venture, there was little glory. By the end of the century his name had become synonymous with bad poetry. Ogilby served as a perfect symbol of the hack, a comprehensive description of the pretender to poetic inspiration. Samuel Wesley humbly remarked, "I can't be angry with any person for ranking me amongst the Ogilbys"[27] and Henry Felton crushingly observed that "perhaps the best way to discern the beauties of good writing is to read some of the worst. Ogilby and Dryden will show you the difference, and when you perceive the insufferable dullness of the one, you will see more clearly the brightness of the other."[28] Dryden himself furthered this reputation; for he never mentioned Ogilby without jeers. He appears twice in *MacFlecknoe*, once high in the company of bad writers:

> Let Father Flecknoe fire thy mind with praise
> And Uncle Ogilby thy envy raise.[29]

[27] *An Epistle to a Friend concerning Poetry* (London, 1700), Sig. [A]2r.

[28] *A Dissertation On Reading the Classics* . . . (London, 1730, the fourth edition), pp. 239-40. See also Pope, *Dunciad*, I, 141, 328.

[29] Ll. 173-74; see also ll. 102-3.

In the Preface to *Sylvae* Dryden demanded, "What English readers, unacquainted with Greek or Latin, will believe me, or any other man, when we commend those authors, and confess we derive all that is pardonable in us from their fountains, if they take those to be the same poets whom our Oglebys have translated?"[30]

But in spite of his proclaimed contempt, Dryden did not scorn to borrow when the translation of the erstwhile dancing master helped to fill his needs. No lines were taken verbatim. Ogilby's use lay in furnishing rhymes. In the four Georgics one hundred and five end words clearly derive from his version. They break down into the following distribution: Book I, twenty-two lines; Book II, thirty; Book III, twenty-two; and Book IV, thirty-one. Fifty lines are questionable. It is not clear whether they come from May, Lauderdale, or from other sources.

Overlooking the possibility of a constitutional antipathy to Ogilby's verse, there are several conceivable reasons why Dryden did not use more of "Uncle's" couplets. In the first place, Ogilby's Virgil was the standard translation until it was displaced by Dryden's superb undertaking. However undistinguished his versification and unimaginative his phrases, Ogilby's was the version known to all readers of Virgil in English during the second half of the seventeenth century. Therefore, if Dryden had relied heavily on this object of his scorn, his verses might have had about them the staleness of excessive familiarity.

Second, Ogilby, like Dryden, drew on May to a generous degree. As the second seventeenth-century translator of the *Georgics*, one may say that he set the pattern of borrowing with a difference. He took what he needed—words, phrases, or lines—at the same time adding his own material and his own touch, a touch marked more by a careful literalness than by fine flights of the imagination. As a result, when Dryden needed a rhyme, he frequently had the choice of May or Ogilby. In these cases the end word might be identical, while the remainder of the line showed the individual

---

[30]*Essays of John Dryden*, I, 253. Again, in the Preface to the *Fables*, Dryden wrote, "If [Milbourne] prefers the version of Ogilby to mine, the world has made him the same compliment: for 'tis agreed on all hands, that he writes even below Ogilby. That, you will say, is not easily to be done; . . ." *Ibid.*, II, 271.

touch of the translator. When this choice was present, Dryden, more often than otherwise, swung all the way back to May.[31] It is therefore obvious that many lines which en first glance seem to derive from Ogilby actually derive from *Virgil's Georgicks Englished*. Of course, this may indicate a genuine preference. On the other hand, May's verses were not easily available to the reading public, and his couplets, consequently, had a less hackneyed ring.

A third possible reason for Dryden's neglect (if such it may be called) is that Ogilby's methodical verses were freely used by the gentlemen poets who exercised their poetic talents upon the *Georgics*, but who needed a collection of ready-made rhymes close at hand to speed their labors. Here was the perfect foil. Lauderdale, Addison, and Sedley—to name only a few—often used Ogilby as a base, easily improving on what they found. In his turn Dryden later used the improvements.[32] The result is that we frequently read couplets that seem to be based on Ogilby, but which come, instead, from later translators. This descent with modifications is clearly illustrated in the following couplet: Dryden, III, 397-98: Ogilby, III, 278-79:

> The bristled boar, who feels the pleasant wound,
> Now grinds his arming tusks, and digs the ground.

[31]A typical example of this occurrence is found in Dryden, II, 432-33:
"But when the golden spring reveals the year,
And the white bird returns, whom serpents fear:"
Compare May, II, 349-50:
"But when the golden spring doth first appear
And that white bird returns, whom serpents fear."
And Ogilby, II, 346-47:
"Then set thy vines when the white bird appears
In blushing spring, which the long serpent fears."

[32]An example of this procedure may be found in Dryden, I, 344-45, quoted *supra*. As is there pointed out, Dryden follows Lauderdale. But Lauderdale derives from Ogilby, I, 269-70:
"Hence from no doubtful signs know,
When best to reap, and at what time to sow."
Other examples are: I, Dryden, 307-8/ Ogilby, 231-32/ Lauderdale, 216-17; Dryden, 254-57/ Ogilby, 184-85, 188-89/ Lauderdale, 171-74. Sedley and Addison drew freely on Ogilby, as in the following examples from Book IV: Sedley, 32-33/ Ogilby, 31-32; Sedley, 46-47/ Ogilby, 47-48; Sedley, 104-6/ Addison, 126-27/ Ogilby, 104-5; Sedley, 257-58/ Addison, 311-12/ Ogilby, 258-59. These are only a few illustrations.

Rubbing against a tree, and tears the ground,
Hardning his shoulders 'gainst th'ensuing wound.

Lauderdale, III, 299-300:

Rubbing against a tree he tears the grounds,
And hard'ns his hide against the dint of wounds.

"Anon.," *Examen Poeticum*, 65-66:

The *Sabine boar* does then prepare to wound,
And whets his foamy tusks, and paws the ground:

In these lines we can clearly see that although the later versions are superior, the general rhyme scheme is set by Ogilby. Dryden, for his part, preferred the greater concreteness and vividness of the anonymous poet who wrote the *Examen Poeticum*.[33]

Although the number of rhyme borrowings is not large, Dryden's use of Ogilby's translation falls into the general categories described above in the discussion of Thomas May. Sometimes he uses Ogilby directly and exclusively: Dryden, I, 211-12:

Then toils for beasts, and lime for birds were found,
And deep-mouth dogs did forest walks surround:

Ogilby, I, 148-49:

Then snares for beasts, and lime for birds was found,
And how dogs should the mighty woods surround;[34]

At other times he used the device of combining Ogilby with another translator—in the following example, Lauderdale. Dryden, I, 334-35:

Around our pole the spiry dragon glides,
And like a winding stream the bear divides;

Ogilby, I, 259-60:

Here round about the mighty serpent glides,
And like a river the two bears divides

Lauderdale, 244-45:

[33]For a general discussion of this version, see below, pp. 300-304.

[34]A few examples, taken from Book IV, are: Dryden, 14-15/ Ogilby, 13-14; Dryden, 43-44/ Ogilby, 35-36; Dryden, 124/ Ogilby, 94; Dryden, 135-36/ Ogilby, 100-2; Dryden, 165/ Ogilby, 122.

Round this, the dragon's spiral volume glide,
Which, river-like, the *Northern bears* divide,[35]

Clearly the principal contribution of this pedestrian poet lay in speeding a greater translator's labors.

Abraham Cowley

Cowley's "Praise of a Country Life," which is a translation of part of the Second Georgic, appears in his essay *Of Agriculture*. There is no way of setting the date of composition. Sprat assures us that the *Essays* are, "The last pieces that we have from his [Cowley's] hands . . ."[36] However Professor A. B. Gough modifies this judgment, observing, "The translations and original poems appended to, or inserted in some of the essays, were, at least in part, written independently of them."[37] The date of composition is therefore uncertain. We can only be sure that the translation is no later than 1667 (the date of Cowley's death). Cowley's rendering is remarkable for its slight resemblance to May and Ogilby.

Twice, at least, Dryden mentioned this piece of work. The first reference is in the Dedication of the *Æneis*, where he writes, "Some of our countrymen have translated episodes and other parts of Virgil with great success; . . . I say nothing of Sir John Denham, Mr Waller, and Mr Cowley; 'tis the utmost of my ambition to be thought their equal, or not to be much inferior to them. . . ."[38] By the time he reached the Postscript his enthusiasm seems to have waned; for he remarks that, "Mr Cowley's *Praise of a Country Life* is excellent, but it is rather an imitation of Virgil than a version."[39] In spite of these qualifications, at least twenty of Cowley's lines have their echoes in Dryden. One line is used verbatim. It appears in conjunction with a rhyme scheme based on Cowley. Dryden, II, 671-72:

[35]Other examples are: II, Dryden, 645-46/ Ogilby, 506/ Cowley, 645; III, Dryden, 748-50/ Ogilby, 533-34/ May, 451-52.
[36]*An Account of the Life of Mr Abraham Cowley*, Sig. dᵛ.
[37]*The Essays and Other Prose Writings* (1915), p. 311.
[38]Ker, *op. cit.*, II, 222.
[39]*Ibid.*, p. 244.

From hence Astræa took her flight; and here
The prints of her departing steps appear.

Cowley, 664-65:

From hence Astræa took her flight, and here
Still her last foot-steps upon earth appear.

In one couplet we find a combination of Ogilby and Cowley.

Dryden, II, 645-46:

With eager eyes, devouring as they pass,
The breathing figures of Corinthian brass.

Cowley, 645-46:

Adoring the rich figures as they pass,
In tap'stry wrought, or cut in living brass

Ogilby, 506:

Gold woven vestments, nor Corinthian brass.

Here Dryden's couplet is fundamentally based on Cowley. However, the greater explicitness of Ogilby's "Corinthian brass" probably explains the source of this term, although there is ample authority in the text, the *Interpretatio*, and the *Notæ* of the Dauphin edition.[40]

There are also a few places where Dryden has combined May and Cowley. Dryden, II, 777-78:

Such was the life the frugal Sabines led;
So Remus and his brother god were bred:

May, II, 581-82:

Such lives as this the ancient Sabines led
And so were Romulus and Remus bred;

Cowley, 748, 750:

Such was the life the prudent Sabines chose,

.   .   .   .

Such, Remus and the god his brother led,

In this couplet Dryden apparently chose to follow Cowley in all but the rhyme, which is based on May. Particularly striking is line 778, where with only slight modification Dryden has used

[40]Cf. also II, Dryden, 692/ Ogilby, 515/ and Cowley, 685.

Cowley's phrase, "the god his brother," a figure we find neither
in Virgil nor in May.[41] Usually, however, Dryden does not mix
his Cowley, preferring to use him straight. Dryden, II, 651-52:

> He boasts no wool whose native white is dyed
> With purple poison of Assyrian pride

Cowley, 647-48:

> Nor is his wool superfluously dy'd
> With the dear poison of *Assyrian* pride.[42]

His main use is as a maker of rhyme schemes, affording Dryden
an easy means of concluding his work on Book II. Incidentally,
there are four lines which, in their different interpretations, afford
an amusing contrast in point of view, particularly if one remembers
the story that toward the end of Cowley's life he grew to dislike
women so intensely that he left the room if one entered. With
that biographical detail in mind, the following lines speak for themselves. Dryden, II, 759-62:

> His cares are eas'd with intervals of bliss:
> His little children, climbing for a kiss,
> Welcome their father's late return at night;
> His faithful bed is crown'd with chaste delight.

Cowley, 736-39:

> He meets at door the softest humane blisses,
> His chast wives welcome, and dear childrens' kisses.
> When any rural holidays invite
> His genius forth to innocent delight.

Richard Maitland, Earl of Lauderdale

With the Earl of Lauderdale we come to the first translator to
whom Dryden indicated in any way the extent of his indebtedness.
In his dedication to the *Æneis* he wrote, "The late Earl of Lauderdale sent me over his new translation of the *Æneis*, which he had
ended before I engag'd in the same design . . . He resolv'd to have
printed his work; which he might have done two years before I

[41] *Vide Georgics*, II, 532-33. Another example of Dryden's use of May and
Cowley occurs in II, Dryden, 734-35/ May, 549-51/ Cowley, 712-13.

[42] In addition, cf. II, Dryden, 654/ Cowley, 650; Dryden, 662/ Cowley, 655;
Dryden, 666/ Cowley, 657; Dryden, 687/ Cowley, 678; Dryden, 717/ Cowley,
700; Dryden, 745-46/ Cowley, 724-25; Dryden, 763-64/ Cowley, 732-33.

could publish mine; and had performed it, if death had not prevented him. But having his manuscript in my hands, I consulted it
as often as I doubted my author's sense; for no man understood
Virgil better than that learned nobleman."[43] A comparison of their
translations clearly establishes the fact that Lauderdale sent over
not only his *Æneis;* he also sent over his *Georgics.* Among all the
English versions represented in Dryden's *Georgics,* Lauderdale is
first, leading May by a very slight margin.

Dryden's association with Lauderdale dated from at least 1682.
According to a manuscript biography written by Knightly Chet-
wood, Dean of Gloucester, in that year the Earl of Roscommon set
about organizing a literary academy, inspired by one which had
been formed at Caen thirty years previously. In addition to Roscommon the membership included the Marquis of Halifax; William,
Lord Cavendish (probably later the first Duke of Devonshire);
Lord Buckhurst, later the Earl of Dorset; Sir Charles Scarborough;
Heneage Finch; John Dryden, the poet laureate; and, "The Lord
Maitland . . . who then began his excellent translation of Virgil."[44]
It is impossible to say whether or not Lauderdale was working on
the *Georgics* at this time. We do know, as his translation in *Sylvae*
testifies, that part of Book IV was available for publication in 1685.

There were two easily available places where Dryden could turn
whenever he wanted to consult Lauderdale. The first as we know
was his friend's manuscript. The second was in the Miscellanies,
where there are two printed excerpts. This second source introduces
an interesting bibliographical point that has previously been overlooked. Taken chronologically, the first of Lauderdale's printed
excerpts deals with the incident of Orpheus and Eurydice. For
many years it has been persistently and wrongly attributed to
Thomas Creech. This error can be explained by the fact that it was
first published in *Sylvae* under the title, "Part of Virgils 4th
Georgick, Englished by an unknown Hand."[45] The poem which

[43]Ker, *op. cit.,* II, 235.

[44]All the preceding information is based on Carl Niemeyer, "The Earl of
Roscommon's Academy," *Modern Language Notes,* XLIV (1934), 432-37; see
a note by the same author, also dealing with this subject, in *Harvard Summaries*
(1933), 290-93.

[45]*Sylvae* (1685), pp. 145-54.

immediately precedes it is by Creech. By the time the Miscellany had reached a fourth edition the original translation by Creech had been omitted and Lauderdale's anonymous version had been added to Creech's canon.[46] This error of ascription has persisted, having been repeated only recently.[47] Actually, the section in question is lines 491-637 of Lauderdale's translation.[48]

The second selection appeared nine years later—one year before its author's death—in *The Annual Miscellany* for 1694.[49] It is listed as "The First Book of Virgil's Georgicks. Translated into English Verse by the Right Honourable John Earl of Lauderdale." It is thus wrongly ascribed to John, probably the famous second Earl of Lauderdale, the secretary of state and the uncle of Richard Maitland, Dryden's associate.

Like his fellow translators, Lauderdale leaned heavily on May and Ogilby, often improving their lines rather than altering them materially. For this reason it is sometimes very difficult to determine precisely to whom Dryden was indebted. It would be altogether unjust, however, to dismiss Lauderdale with the suggestion that he is the creature of his predecessors. Many of his passages altogether surpass their work, both in originality and poetic feeling. Of these Dryden was fully aware. Take, for example, the following adaptation. Dryden, I, 272-73:

> Mark well the flowering almonds in the wood;
> If od'rous blooms the bearing branches load,

Lauderdale, I, 185-86:

> Consider well the almonds in the wood,
> If buds and flow'rs the frangrant branches load.

In addition to its greater charm, Lauderdale's translation is more fluent than were the performances of May and Ogilby. His work is smoother, tighter, and more polished. The most cursory com-

[46]"Part of Virgils IV Georgick. By Mr Creech," in *The Second Part of Miscellany Poems* ... The Fourth Edition ... (MDCCVI), pp. 215-19. I have not been able to check the second and third editions.

[47]Dwight L. Durling, *Georgic Tradition in English Poetry* (New York, 1935), p. 219.

[48]Lauderdale's version was not published *in toto* until 1718.

[49]Pp. 217-53.

parison affords a striking proof of the technical developments achieved in the heroic couplet between 1628, when May's version was published, and the '80s, when Lauderdale worked on his.

Dryden's borrowings fall into the general patterns already discussed in connection with May and Ogilby. There is the use of nearly identical lines. Dryden, I, 195: "For all was common, and the fruitful earth." Lauderdale, I, 124: "For all lay common, and the fruitful earth."[50]

The following quotation affords a composite illustration of the uses to which Dryden put Lauderdale—liberal modification, with only the rhyme words used in order to facilitate the production of a couplet; slight modification, with the line remaining basically as Lauderdale wrote it; and verbatim borrowing. Dryden, I, 379-86:

> The sev'nth is, next the tenth, the best to join
> Young oxen to the yoke, and plant the vine.
> Then weavers stretch your stays upon the weft:
> The ninth is good for travel, bad for theft.
> Some works in dead of night are better done;
> Or when the morning dew prevents the sun.
> Parch'd mead and stubble now, by Phoebe's light;
> When both require the coolness of the night.

Lauderdale, I, 286-93:

> Next to the tenth, the sev'nth to plant the vine
> Is lucky, then unbroken bullocks join;
> Then weavers stretch your stays upon the waft
> The ninth for trav'ling's good, and ill for theft.
>   Some works by cool of night are better done,
> Or when the dew prevents the rising sun;[51]
> Parch'd meadows, and dry stubble mow by night,
> Then moisture reigns, which flies Apollo's light.[52]

[50]For other examples, see: I, Dryden, 364/ Lauderdale, 271; Dryden, 330-31/ Lauderdale, 240-41; Dryden, 344-45/ Lauderdale, 252-53; Dryden, 281/ Lauderdale, 190.

[51]Cf. Ogilby, I, 307-8:
"Many works better in cold night are done,
Or when the pearly morning brings the sun."

[52]For other examples of Dryden's use of extended passages in Lauderdale, see I, Dryden, 292-97/ Lauderdale, 201-7; Dryden, 367-68, 371-74/ Lauderdale, 274-79; Dryden, 391-94/ Lauderdale, 295-99; Dryden, 407-10/ Lauderdale, 307-11; Dryden, 672-75/ Lauderdale, 559-62. There are many more such illustrations.

There are passages in which one finds both May and Lauderdale, as in the following four lines—Dryden, I, 219-22:

> First Ceres taught, the ground with grain to sow
> And arm'd with iron shares the crooked plough;
> When now Dodonian oaks no more supply'd
> Their mast, and trees their forest-fruit deny'd.

The basic rhymes for these two pairs of couplets are—May, I, 152-53:

> First yellow Ceres taught the world to plow
> When woods no longer could afford enow.

and Lauderdale, I, 145-46:

> When to mankind *Dodona* aid deny'd,
> Nor fruit, nor acorns for their food supply'd,[53]

Last and most frequent, there are places where Dryden uses Lauderdale's rhyme words alone, characteristically revising the remainder of the line to suit himself. Dryden, I, 179-80:

> But glutton geese, and the Strymonian crane,
> With foreign birds, invade the tender grain.

Lauderdale, I, 116-17:

> The bitter endive's shade, Strymonian cranes,
> And rav'nous geese are hurtful to the grains.

In short, his use of Lauderdale is so extensive that it is impossible to indicate more than briefly its variety and scope. Recapitulated, the figures follow: a total of 241 rhyme words—Book I, 110; Book II, 25; Book III, 50; and Book IV, 56. Dryden uses 5 identical lines, all in Book I. In addition, there are 42 questionable lines—2 in Book I; 7 in Book II; 10 in Book III; and 23 in Book IV. In company with Thomas May, Lauderdale served very much as a skeleton for the rhyme scheme of his friend's translation.

[53]For other combinations of May and Lauderdale, *vide* I, Dryden, 175-81/ May, 139-40/ Lauderdale, 134-37. In the extended quotation comprising Dryden, I, 264-71, there are three different sources for the rhymes; they break down as follows: Dryden, 264-65/ May, 185; Dryden, 268-69/ Ogilby, 195-96/ Dryden, 270-71/ Lauderdale, 183-84.

John Sheffield, Duke of Buckingham and Normanby

Dryden's version of lines 683-84 of Book IV reads,

> Men, matrons, children, and th'unmarried maid,
> The mighty heroes more majestic shade.

Since its publication in the first edition, line 684 has always been footnoted: "This whole line is taken from the Marquess of Normanby's translation." The reference—notable because it is the only place in the *Georgics* where Dryden acknowledges indebtedness to a specific line—is to Normanby's translation of "Part of Virgil's Fourth Georgick," the story of Orpheus and Eurydice, first published in the *Miscellany* of 1684. Lines 23-24 read,

> Matrons and men, raw youths and unripe maids,
> And mighty heroes more majestic shades.

The similarity of the two versions is clearly evident. Echoes of Normanby in the remainder of the episode are very small indeed. In addition to the two lines just quoted, line 763 resembles, in rhyme word at least, line 77 in Normanby. Line 687 is perhaps derived from line 27, but this is questionable. Thus, we have a total of three lines based on Normanby, and one where attribution is not certain.

Of course, Dryden may have been impressed by the material he modified. However, there is also a possibility that he was acknowledging a wealthy association that dated back to at least 1676, when he dedicated *Aureng-Zebe* to Normanby, then the Earl of Mulgrave. Five years later, in "Absolom and Achitophel," he referred to his patron as, "Sharp-judging Adriel, the Muse's friend."[54] Again, in the lines "To the Earl of Roscommon on his Excellent Essay on Translated Verse" (1684), Mulgrave was mentioned as the translator of the Ovidian epistle "Helen to Paris"[55]—actually a reference to the version made by Mulgrave and Dryden. The climax to these years of patronage came in 1697, when Dryden dedicated

[54]Line 877.

[55]Ll. 59-62. *The Letterbook of Sir George Etherege* (ed. Sybil Rosenfeld, 1928), contains a letter from Mulgrave to Etherege, dated March 7, 1687, which begins, "I saw t'other day by chance a letter of yours to Mr Dryden . . ." (p. 357). This unquestionably indicates continued friendship at this time between the two men.

the *Æneis* to Normanby.[56] Here is evidence of over twenty years' association that was both literary and remunerative in its aspects. This is why it is tempting to argue that Dryden's very small use of Normanby's translation was in the nature of a complimentary gesture to a nobleman who affected literary taste, rather than an indication of poetic aid that could not be got elsewhere.

Knightly Chetwood

Dr. Knightly Chetwood is referred to in the dedication of the *Æneis*, where Dryden speaks of the work of two "worthy friends of mine, who desire to have their names conceal'd."[57] Chetwood was one of them, having contributed the "Life of Virgil" and the Preface to the "Pastorals" to the undertaking.[58] In the notes to Georgic II Dryden writes that, "*The Praises of Italy* (translated by the learned and every way excellent Mr Chetwood), which are printed in one of my *Miscellany Poems*, are the greatest ornament of the book." This is a reference to the sixty-seven line version of the passage beginning, "*Sed neque Medorum sylvae, ditissima terra*,"[59] which appeared in the *Miscellany Poems* of 1684. After such praise one might well expect to find that Dryden had availed himself of his friend's translation. Anyone who looks for extensive borrowings is doomed to disappointment. Furthermore, the number of lines that can be traced to Chetwood is small, uncertain, and unimportant. At the very most the indebtedness amounts to five lines; at the least, one. Three lines are in question because of the uncertainty of knowing when the Lauderdale version was finished. Therefore, we cannot say who used whom.[60] In any case, Chetwood was thoroughly familiar with May and Ogilby and he made good use of them. As a result, what frequently seems to be a corres-

[56]Years later Normanby, then the Duke of Buckingham, erected the monument over Dryden's neglected grave.

[57]Ker, *op. cit.*, II, 235.

[58]*Ibid.*, p. 306.

[59]Virgil, ll. 136 ff. The equivalent portion of Dryden's translation begins at l. 187.

[60]Cf. II, Dryden, 227-28/ Chetwood, 46-47/ Lauderdale, 210; there is a pronounced similarity, but the lack of evidence concerning the date of composition of the Chetwood and Lauderdale versions makes speculation on derivation useless.

pondence between Dryden and Chetwood often turns out to be
something that both men could have got from a third source. Thus,
at first glance one could make a thoroughly plausible case for
Dryden's use of Chetwood in the following couplet: Dryden, II,
221-22:

> Or shall I praise thy ports, or mention make
> Of the vast mound, that binds the Lucrine lake.

Chetwood, 40-41:

> What should I tell how Art cou'd undertake
> To make a Haven in the *Lucrine* lake?

However, the line from May (II, 176) tempers one's partisanship:
"Or praise her havens? or the Lucrine Lake?" All we can say
with certainty is that Chetwood used May. But whether Dryden
stemmed from one or both when he devised the rhyme scheme for
these two lines, is in the province of uncertain speculation.[61]

Only one line can be traced to Chetwood with certainty, and
here only a rhyme word is used, the rest being Dryden. Dryden,
II, 215-16:

> Our forts on sleepy hills, that far below
> See wanton streams, in winding valleys flow.

Chetwood, 32-33:

> There, big with story, ancient walls do show
> Their reverend heads; beneath fam'd rivers flow.

In the face of this trifling evidence concerning Dryden's high re-
gard for Chetwood's work, we are left with a choice of two conclusions: Either Dryden showed remarkable restraint in not using
more material from a translation he assertedly admired—a demon-
stration of self-denial not borne out by practice elsewhere—or we

---

[61]Other questionable lines (all references to Book II) are: Dryden, 187-88/
Lauderdale, 171-72/ Chetwood, 3-4. Dryden, 245-46 is probably Ogilby, 193-94,
with a touch of Lauderdale, 226-27; the rhyme scheme, which was originally set
by May, was followed by Chetwood, 67. Cf. also Dryden, 219, and Chetwood, 38,
for a similarity in phraseology.

must conclude that Dryden's high praise was in the nature of grateful thanks and compliment to an old friend who had done yeoman service in the preparation of the Virgil.

The Anonymous Translator of "Amor omnibus idem."

In the Postscript to the Virgil Dryden wrote, "Whoever has given the world the translation of part of the Third *Georgic*, which he calls *The Power of Love*, has put me to sufficient pains to make my own not inferior to his."[62] He was here referring to the anonymous translation, "*Amor omnibus idem;* or, The Force of Love in All Creatures, being a translation of some verses in Virgil's Third Georgic, from verse 209 to verse 285," which appeared in *Examen Poeticum*, the third Miscellany, in 1693. Commenting on these remarks, Malone observed, "From the high praise he has given to these verses, which greatly exceeds their merit, I suspect that the concealed translator was our author's friend, George Granville, later Lord Lansdowne."[63] Malone's guess is based on the fact that the poem immediately preceding "*Amor omnibus idem*" is Granville's "Imitation of the 2d Chorus in the second Act of Seneca's Thyestes." He offers no stronger evidence. But as we have already seen in the case of the erroneous ascription of Lauderdale's verses to Creech, such testimony is far from conclusive. Granville's collected works give no hint that he undertook this translation. Furthermore, his most recent biographer does not include it in her list of Granville's poems published in the third Miscellany.[64] Therefore, until proof of a more telling nature is presented, Malone's hypothesis must be considered unproved, and the author of these lines still classified as anonymous.

Not only is the authorship unknown, but the date of composition is equally obscure. All that we know is the *terminus ad quem,* 1693, afforded by the publication of the *Examen Poeticum*. The verse is sufficiently smooth and tight to indicate that without doubt

[62]Ker,*op. cit.,* II, 244.

[63]Edmund Malone, *The Critical and Miscellaneous Prose Works of John Dryden,* III (MDCCC), 564.

[64]Elizabeth Handasyde, *Granville the Polite* (1933), p. 278.

it was written some time after the translations of May and Ogilby, with whose work the unknown translator was indisputably familiar. There are also marked resemblances to Lauderdale. Unfortunately for the symmetrical beauty of a water-tight chronology, it is impossible to say whether the version in *Examen Poeticum* or the Lauderdale rendering was made first, and who, therefore, was the borrower.

Professor Noyes has pointed out that Dryden "fails to state that from this piece he took three whole lines (ll. 402, 431 and 448) and suggestions for many others, for his own translation."[65] In the main he is quite right. Dryden did not scruple to use the version wherever it would help. According to my count, Dryden took from this source sixteen rhyme words, three identical lines, and one line very nearly identical. Four other lines involving the use of rhyme words are questionable; they are common to several sources, any of which Dryden might have used. However, examination of many of the lines in question reveals that even here, where Dryden relied heavily on one man, he kept to his usual practice of taking a phrase from one, a hint from a second, a suggestion from a third, while adding to the entire production a liberal helping of that dash and vigor that makes his Virgil one of the great English translations. As is shown below, some of the lines that Dryden adapted from the version in the *Examen Poeticum* follow a direction already set by May and Ogilby. One must again point out that it is never safe to assume that Dryden borrowed from a specific source until all versions have been compared. Thus at first glance there seems to be every reason for arguing a relationship between the two following couplets from Book III. Dryden, 365-66:

> Then, to redeem his honour at a blow,
> He moves his camp, to meet his careless foe.

Ex. Poet. 38-39:

> Then with his force and strength prepar'd does go
> With headlong rage against th'unwary foe:

[65] *The Poetical Works of John Dryden*, ed. G. R. Noyes (1909), pp. 1000-1.

However, May's version (284-85) seems closer to Dryden than does this middle source:

> And well improv'd, he doth with fury go
> To meet again his not forgotten foe.[66]

In Dryden's translation of the following lines we find again evidences of a combination of several translators. Dryden, III, 356-59:

> Hardning his limbs with painful exercise,
> And rough upon the flinty rock he lies.
> On prickly leaves, and on sharp herbs he feeds,
> Then to the prelude of a war proceeds.

May, III, 276-79:

> Then he with care his strength doth exercise;
> Upon the hardest stones all night he lies
> On roughest leaves, and sharpest herbs he feeds,
> Oft tryes himself; with wrathful horns proceeds

Lauderdale, III, 267-68:

> All night he lies on the cold rocks, and feeds
> On prickly leaves, on fenny sedge and reeds:

Ex. Poet., 30-32:

> Then with redoubled care his strength supplies,
> Rough on the flinty ground all night he lies,
> And shrubs, and prickling thistles for his food suffice

Analysis shows that the end word of line 356 is from May, Dryden having changed it from a verb to a noun. Line 357 closely follows *Examen Poeticum*. Line 358 is a combination of line 268 in Lauderdale and line 278 in May. And last of all, line 359 corresponds with May, line 279, as far as the end word is concerned.

---

[66]In this connection it is well to remember that the anonymous translator was also familiar with John Ogilby. Professor Noyes points out a certain resemblance between Dryden, 408, "And rolling thunder rattled o'er his head," and *Ex. Poet.*, 73-74:

> "Whilst from the throne
> Of Heav'n its loud artillery rattles down
> On his devoted head; Nor can the sound ... "

Compare this with Ogilby, 285-86:

> "When at him Heaven's artillery thundred round,
> And broken billows 'gainst the rocks resound:"

Now let us examine a passage where Dryden relies primarily on *Examen Poeticum*. In the following six-line quotation Dryden bases his first four on the *Miscellany* version, turning for the last two to Lauderdale. Dryden, III, 428-33:

> When at the spring's approach their marrow burns,
> (For with the spring their genial warmth returns)
> The mares to cliffs of rugged rocks repair,
> And with wide nostrils snuff the western air:
> Where (wondrous to relate!) the parent wind,
> Without the stallion, propagates the kind.

Compare Dryden's lines with the following versions, culminating with the *Examen Poeticum*. May, III, 323-24:

> And when love's flame their greedy marrows burns
> Most in the spring (for heat then most returns)

Ogilby, III, 296-97:

> And straight with hidden fire their marrow burns:
> But most i' the spring, when heat of blood returns;

Lauderdale, III, 320-25:

> In spring their love with greater ardor burns,
> When to their bones prolific warmth returns:
> On pointed cliffs they gape, and westward stare,
> To meet the god who breathes a wanton air.
> Thus, though it's wondrous strange, yet oft we find
> Mares without males impregnate by the wind;

Ex. Poet., 92-95:

> When spring's soft fire their melting marrow burns
> (For 'tis in Spring the lusty warmth returns)
> They to the tops of steepest hills repair,
> And with wide nostrils snuff the western air.

The line of descent in the five different translations is perfectly obvious. Dryden relied on two sources—on *Examen Poeticum* for lines 428-30, while line 431 is incorporated verbatim from this same source. In lines 432-33 the resemblance to Lauderdale is not difficult to perceive, although Dryden here merely used a rhyme word to help himself along. An additional point should be considered, and that is the general resemblance in all the versions of the first

couplet in this passage. May gave it its first form. Ogilby modified
it, while keeping its general structure and rhyme scheme. Lauderdale and the anonymous translator, each in turn, added his touch,
and the two lines were given their final form by Dryden. Here is
one more example of a process no longer striking—the principle
of genealogy in seventeenth-century translations of Virgil.

Henry Sacheverell

The *Third Part of the Miscellany* (1693) contains a translation
listed as "Part of Virgils first Georgick, Translated into English
Verse by Henry Sacheverill,"[67] which is dedicated to Dryden.
Perhaps recognition of this compliment explains the following
similarity—Dryden, I, 472: "And milk and honey, mix with spark-
ling wine;" Sacheverill, 6: "With milk, with honey, and with flow-
ing wine." There is no further correspondence between the two
versions.[68]

Joseph Addison

Addison's "Translation of all Virgils Fourth Georgick, except
the Story of Aristeus" appeared in the *Annual Miscellany* for
1694.[69] In the "Postscript to the Reader," appended to the *Georgics*,
Dryden took special pains to mention Addison's work, indicating
that its excellence had served as a spur to his own efforts. "The
most ingenious Mr. Addison has also been as troublesome to me as
the other two [i.e. the anonymous translator of *Amor omnibus
idem* and Lord Roscommon's translation of *Silenus*], and on the
same account. After his *Bees*, my latter swarm is scarcely worth
the hiving."[70] From this high praise we might reasonably expect a

---

[67]Generally accepted as Henry Sacheverell, in later years the eminent Tory
divine.

[68]Dryden, I, 501-4/ Lauderdale, I, 382-85/ Ogilby, I, 390-92/ and Sacheverell,
60-61 are worth examining. Phrases peculiar, on one hand, to Dryden and Lauderdale, and on the other to Ogilby and Sacheverell show that while the rhyme words
are the same, Dryden used Lauderdale, while Sacheverell derived from Ogilby.

[69]Pp. 58-86.

[70]Ker, *op. cit.*, p. 244.

considerable reliance on Addison's translation. Actually, Dryden used it only a little more than he did Cowley's. According to my figures, twenty end-words, one line verbatim, and ten questionable end-words (that is, they might have come from Ogilby, on whom Addison leaned heavily, or they might have come from Sedley) form the sum total of indebtedness.

Briefly reviewing Dryden's use of Addison, let us first examine the one verbatim line. Dryden, IV, 445-46:

> Or flights of arrows from the Parthian bows,
> When from afar they gall embattled foes;

Addison, 419-20:

> Or flights of arrows from the Parthian bows,
> When twanging strings first shoot 'em on the foes.[71]

In the couplets where Dryden utilized rhyme words only, the following is a fair sample. Dryden, IV, 295-96:

> And thus their little citizens create
> And waxen cities build, and palaces of state.

Addison, 277-78:

> From these they choose out subjects, and create
> A little monarch of the rising state.[72]

An example of combinations of Addison with his predecessors is found in Dryden, IV, 23-24:

> But near a living stream their mansion place,
> Edg'd round with moss, and tufts of matted grass:

May, IV, 21-22:

> Green mossy fountains still your bee-hives place,
> And streams that glide along the verdant grass,

[71]The ancestor of both couplets is Lauderdale, IV, 353-54:
"Or flights of arrows from the twanging bows,
When light arm'd Parthians first attack the foes."

[72]Other examples of this practice are: IV, Dryden, 12-13/ Addison, 12-13; Dryden, 358-59/ Ogilby, 276-77/ Addison, 333-34 (here the ancestor is Ogilby, but Dryden used Addison); Dryden, 316/ Addison, 297; Dryden, 423-24/ Addison, 398-99.

Ogilby, IV, 21-22:

> But their abodes, near crystal fountains, place,
> Where purling streams glide gently through the grass,

Addison, 22-23:

> Let purling streams, and fountains edg'd with moss,
> And shallow rills run trickling through the grass.

In Dryden's couplet the rhyme scheme follows May and Ogilby, rather than Addison. As is so often the case, the inner part of the two lines bears Dryden's own individual twist. However, not only can we trace May and Ogilby, but Addison's version has its echoes here also. In line 24 Addison's moss figure (see Addison, line 23) is used, having been taken out of its focal position of rhyme phrase and placed at the beginning of the line.[73]

Dryden's borrowings from Addison's translation of Book IV are not fundamental or important, and do not contribute materially to the progress of this part of the *Georgics*. In spite of his expressions of admiration and, one might almost say, of envy for the felicity of his young friend's version, the use Dryden found for it was slight and of a nature that might easily have been found elsewhere.

Sir Charles Sedley

The last piece of work considered here is Sir Charles Sedley's translation of Book IV. Unfortunately, the date of composition is unknown. Until that information is available, very little can be said about it; consequently, this brief statement is added as an appendix to the main discussion.

Sedley's version runs to 627 lines, and contains resemblances to almost every other rendition of the Fourth Book that has been listed. We can safely say that he drew heavily on May and Ogilby. But until we know whether his *Georgic* is the product of his youth, when he translated Ovid, or of his old age when he translated Horace,[74] we cannot with certainty say whether he originated or

[73]For another illustration of combination, see IV, Dryden, 234-36/ May, 187-89/ Ogilby, 181-83/ Addison, 212-14.

[74]*The Poetical and Dramatic Works of Sir Charles Sedley*, ed. V. De Sola Pinto, I, (1928), xvii.

echoed the considerable number of rhyme words and phrases common to him and Lauderdale, Mulgrave, and Addison. He is included
here because there are also correspondences peculiar only to him
and Dryden.

The translation was first published posthumously, when Ayloffe
included it in his edition of Sedley's *Poetical Works*.[75] Professor
De Sola Pinto, Sedley's only modern biographer and editor, thinks
that certain roughnesses in the version indicate that it was left in an
unfinished state. As to the possible priority of Dryden or Sedley, he
is noncommittal. In his biographical study he seems to lean toward
an early date for Sedley, pointing out that the verse is characterized
by a greater flexibility because of his use of the " 'overflowing'
couplet instead of the strictly stopped form, which was becoming
increasingly popular at the end of the seventeenth century."[76] In
his edition of Sedley's works he remarks, "As the date of Sedley's
version is unknown, it is impossible to know whether he or Dryden
is the borrower."[77]

Regardless of the date of composition, the fact remains that at
least twenty lines find echoes in Sedley and Dryden and nowhere
else. Illustrative of this type of similarity is Dryden, IV, 541: "And
thus, at length, in human accent spoke"; Sedley, 486: "And with a
human voice at last he spoke."
Another is Dryden, IV, 337-38:

> Two honey harvests fall in every year:
> First, when the pleasing Pleides appear,

Sedley, 258-59:

> Twice they have young, two harvests in a year,
> Once when the lovely Pleides appear.[78]

In the following four lines Dryden's first couplet follows the
rhyme scheme of three other versions. The second couplet, however,
corresponds with Sedley alone. Dryden, IV, 59-62:

[75]London, 1702.
[76]*Sir Charles Sedley, 1639-1701* (1927), p. 300.
[77]*The Poetical and Dramatic Works*, I, 293.
[78]Already quoted, *supra*, p. 278, are Dryden, IV, 390 and Sedley, 300. Other
examples are: Dryden, 91-92/ Sedley, 78-79; Dryden, 297/ Sedley, 229; Dryden,
411/ Sedley, 322; Dryden, 695/ Sedley, 530; Dryden, 706-7/ Sedley, 540-41.

Nor bees are lodg'd in hives alone, but found
In chambers of their own, beneath the ground:
Their vaulted roofs are hung in pumices,
And in the rotten trunks of hollow trees.

May, IV, 56-57:

.   .   .   ; and under ground
(If fame speak truly) bees have oft been found

Lauderdale, IV, 50-51:

For oft the bees (if Fame be true) are found
To dig themselves a lodging under ground;

Sedley, 48-51:

If Fame say true, sometimes they under ground
Make themselves nests, sometimes their swarms are found
In the dark vaults of hollow pumices,
Or in the rotten trunks of aged trees.

The searcher for lines identical in the two translations must be content with only one. Dryden, IV, 479, and Sedley, 373, both read: "*Cydipe* and *Lycoras*, one a maid."[79] Further speculation about the two translations is blocked because of the lack of available information. Some day soon, perhaps, a scholar will unearth the date of Sedley's version. Whoever finds it will clarify a baffling point in the chronology of seventeenth-century Virgil studies.

IV

The evidence presented in the preceding pages makes it abundantly clear that Dryden was familiar with the previous English rhymed translations of the *Georgics*. Of the nine (and possibly ten) versions which Dryden used, he borrowed most extensively from Lauderdale and May. With the exception of Lauderdale, he borrows most freely from translators whom he either does not mention or mentions deprecatingly. He makes little use of Normanby, Chetwood, and Addison, whom he makes a point of praising.

[79]Derived from May, IV, 387.

Mr. Bottkol's study of Dryden's use of Latin texts and commentaries is essential for an understanding of Dryden's art of translation, but no valid conclusions can be drawn from such a method until the poet's indebtedness to his English predecessors is known. Mr. Bottkol employs his apparatus laboriously to show that in I, 570, the line "From hence the cows exult, and frisking lambs rejoice" is a disfiguring of the poet's meaning, "cows" being an absurd typographical error for "crows." An examination of Dryden's predecessors would have pointed to the misprint; for Ogilby and Lauderdale indentified the exulting animals as "crows" and "rooks" respectively.[80]

The question arises, why did Dryden, who wrote so easily and who wrote so well, borrow so much from his relatively negligible predecessors? The answer is suggested by Dryden's own words. In the Dedication of the *Æneis* he says, "From the beginning of the First Georgic to the end of the last Æneid, I found the difficulty of translation growing on me in every succeeding book. For Virgil, above all poets, had a stock which I may call almost inexhaustible, of figurative, elegant, and sounding words: I . . . have found it very painful to vary words, when the same sense returns upon me . . . Words are not so easily coined as money; and yet we see that the credit not only of banks but of exchequers cracks when little comes in, and much goes out."[81]

It is notable that Dryden takes over few whole lines or couplets verbatim from his predecessors. By far the greatest part of his borrowings are confined to rhyme words and phrases. This fact suggests that Dryden was glad to dispense with the drudgery of rhyming, preferring to spend his talents on the creation of poetry. Out of the 3,149 lines in Dryden's *Georgics*, the poet took over 20 per cent of the rhyme words directly from his predecessors (and this does not count those instances in which Dryden employed a rhyme word obviously suggested by a borrowed rhyme). It appears that his imagination was stimulated by rhyme. Having fixed upon the end word he built easily and gracefully upon it, rendering the

[80]Ogilby, I, 454; Lauderdale, I, 455.

[81]Ker, *op. cit.*, II, 231-32.

sense in the eloquent harmony that is characteristic of his own genius.

Virgil's *Georgics*, Dryden wrote, "I esteem the divinest part of all his writings."[82] With such a respect for his original, Dryden labored to do full justice to the task he undertook. His borrowings are woven into a single fabric, and one needs only to examine his predecessors to discover the superior grace and beauty of that fabric. What was rough, he made smooth; to what was faint and languishing he added revitalizing energy. There is an ease in his line and an inner propulsion in his couplets that are all his own. He borrowed words, but he created poetry.

---

[82]Preface to *Annus Mirabilis, ibid.*, I, 16.

Notes

The Date of "Britannia and Rawleigh"

THE following note on the date of composition of "Britannia and Rawleigh" was prompted by the discovery that no unanimity prevails on the point. G. A. Aitkin[1] thought that the satire was "written at the end of 1673 or early in 1674"; H. M. Margoliouth[2] commented: "Date. Not before 17 December 1674 when Henriette de Quéroualle, younger sister of the Duchess of Portsmouth, married Philip Herbert seventh Earl of Pembroke (see l. 169). 'Long scorned Parliament' (l. 135) suggests some long period of prorogation, for instance that of February 1674-April 1675. A possible date is the early part of 1675, but it may be later. See note on l. 42." Pierre Legouis,[3] without explaining the reason for his choice, assigned the satire to "début de 1675?"

This diversity seems to justify an examination or re-examination of the clues provided by the poem to the time when "Britannia and Rawleigh" was written to see whether a definite conclusion can be reached. In order to avoid forcing the issue, all likely, and some unlikely, interpretations of the clues have been supplied. The reader is given the evidence the writer used in the same order that he uncovered it. The text of H. M. Margoliouth has been cited throughout. To avoid excessive annotations, exact dates have been given for a number of events in order that the reader may, if he wishes, consult the *Journals* of both Houses of Parliament without further reference. No attempt has been made to solve the problem—if there be a problem—of authorship.

[1] *The Muses' Library. Satires of Andrew Marvell* (London: Routledge & Sons ca. 1901), p. 182.

[2] *The Poems & Letters of Andrew Marvell* (Oxford: Clarendon Press, 1927), I, 305. The reference to l. 42, where Spenser is mentioned, is dealt with below.

[3] *André Marvell* (Paris: Henri Didier, 1928), p. 275, n. 187.

Among the most significant lines for present purposes are Britannia's determination not to return to Court

> Till Cavaleers shall favorites be Deem'd
> And loyall sufferings by the Court esteem'd
> Till Howard and Garway shall a bribe reject,
> Till Golden Osborn cheating shall detect,
> Till Atheist Lauderdale shall leave this Land. . . .

At first glance it would appear that if the first two lines have any meaning, they can scarcely be dated later than the spring of 1675 and may well be a year or so ealier. In his speech on the opening of Parliament, April 13, 1675, Charles II made a definite bid for the support of Anglicans and old Cavaliers. In his letter of that day, Andrew Marvell noted that the King had "testified his great satisfaction in this Parliament the most of which had in their own persons or were descended of those who had signalizd themselves in his service," and that he would always maintain the Church of England.[4] In *An Account of Popery and Arbitrary Government*, probably written in 1677 and printed in 1678, Marvell said that ministers "began therefore after fifteen years to remember that there were such a sort of men in England as the old Cavalier party."[5] These passages may not prove, however, that the satirist was writing before April 1675, because other contemporaries make the same kind of remark then as is contained in the two lines quoted above. Thus, during a debate on a Place Bill on April 29, 1675, Sir Charles Wheeler complained that "persons that have been with the King in banishment . . . at the King's return, for want, could not buy places of advantage whilst other men that staid at home, grew rich." Another member, Colonel Strangeways, observes "that few are in office, that formerly have served the King—Neutral persons most."[6] Nevertheless, the change of policy, openly proclaimed in April, 1675, makes improbable a later date for the satire.

"Till Howard and Garway shall a bribe reject . . ."

[4]Margoliouth, II, 140.

[5]*Complete Prose Works*, ed. A. B. Grosart (privately printed 1875) IV, 303; cf. *ibid.*, pp. 261-62.

[6]Anchitell Grey, *Debates of the House of Commons from 1667 to 1694* (London, 1763), III, 53-54. The pagination is confused in my copy of this volume, and the reference is to the repeated pages 53-54.

This line is a direct reference to a vote in the House of Commons on February 7, 1673. During a debate on supply both Sir Robert Howard and William Garroway (Garway) supported a vote to give the Crown £70,000 a month for eighteen months.[7] Howard was attacked on several occasions about this time. In a letter of November, 1670, Howard and four other M.P.'s are said to have deserted the country party in order to "head the King's Busyness." They are called the "five recanters of the Hous" in "Further Advice to a. Painter," and "Fair knights and a knave" in "A Dialogue between Two Horses": and Howard is sarcastically named in "Last Instructions to a Painter."[8] Garroway is favorably noticed in the last satire, but an anecdote recorded in Burnet's *History of My Own Time*,[9] explains why he was held up to execration in "Britannia and Rawleigh." Garroway and Lee, two leaders of the anti-court party, were held to have betrayed their cause when, after a caucus had agreed that only £600,000 should be voted to support the Dutch war, they suddenly proposed £1,200,000 and carried the day. Some versions of this line substitute "Lee" for "Howard," and this change makes the meter better and the references more obvious. As there appears to be no other blot on Garroway's career,[10] the supposition is not unreasonable that the line under discussion was written fairly soon after his surprising vote in the Commons.

"Till Golden Osborn cheating shall detect . . ." is a line which suggests a date later than June, 1673, when Sir Thomas Osborne became Lord High Treasurer, but earlier than June, 1674, when he was created Earl of Danby. But the inference is not decisive, for in the Introduction to "A Dialogue between Two Horses," which was written late in 1676, "Osborne" and not "Danby" is introduced, although a few months earlier "Danby" appears in "The Statue at Charing Cross."

"Till Atheist Lauderdale shall leave this Land . . ."

[7]Grey, *Debates* II, 11.

[8]Margoliouth, II, 305; I, 169, 193, 147.

[9]Ed. Osmund Airy (Oxford, 1890), II, 16-17 and 92-93.

[10]His name does not appear in the *Calendar of Treasury Books* of this time, so he did not receive any office of profit and probably did not accept a bribe.

Lauderdale was especially obnoxious to the Commons, because he was alleged to have said that royal edicts were equal to laws and ought to take precedence over them. Accordingly, after a bitter debate on January 13, 1674, an address was voted asking that Lauderdale be removed from His Majesty's presence and councils forever.[11] Charles refused to part with so pliant a minister, and on February 24 prorogued Parliament first to November 10 and then to the following April 13. No sooner did the Houses convene than the Commons fell upon Lauderdale again, and, fortified by Burnet's testimony[12] that Lauderdale had wished the Scottish Presbyterians would rebel so that he might bring Papists from Ireland to cut their throats, presented no less than three addresses against him. Marvell's letters are unusually full of this second attack on Lauderdale,[13] who survived these assaults. In November, Parliament was prorogued and did not meet again until February 1677—a long interval which provoked much adverse comment. Either of these occasions would seem to suit the words in "Britannia and Rawleigh," "Till Charles loves Parliaments . . ." But it is at least possible that an earlier attack on Lauderdale, on October 31, 1673, may have prompted the line, because he was specifically referred to during a debate which preceded a motion that no further supplies would be voted until the kingdom should be free from the dangers of Popish counsels and counsellors.[14] An obstacle to assuming that the line on Lauderdale indicates that the satire was written late in 1674 or early in 1675 or, a fortiori, later still, is the prominent part Garroway took in the Commons against that unpopular minister as early as January, 1674.[15] By the end of this parliamentary session (February 24) Garroway had established his position as a leader of the anti-court party. Surely the satirist would not have branded Garroway after he had adopted in Parliament much the same position as the writer himself. If Marvell was the writer, and penned his satire after February 9, 1674, he was singularly ungracious, for on that day Garroway referred to a book of Dr. Parker's "that

[11]Grey, Debates, II, 236-44; Burnet, II, 44-45 and notes.
[12]Own Time, II, 73-74.
[13]Margoliouth, II, 141, 144-46, etc.
[14]Grey, Debates, II, 197-214.
[15]Grey, Debates, II, 205, 373, 404.

says, 'They are notorious Rebels that shall refuse such a levy made by the King before God.' "[16] Marvell, it will be recalled, had a lively controversy with Samuel Parker.

"The other day fam'd Spencer I did bring . . ."

Mr. Margoliouth has a note that if the reference is to the third folio of Spenser's works advertised in the *Term Catalogues* December 6, 1678, the satire was written after that date and, therefore, after Marvell's death. The poem has no other indication of such late composition. The writer does not seem very familiar with Spenser, for the poet is made responsible for describing

> How, like ripe fruit, she dropt from of the Throne
> Full of Gray Hairs, good deeds, endless renown.

As Spenser died some years before Elizabeth, the passage seems no more than an unlucky affectation of learning and need have no connection at all with the publication of the third folio.

The satire has nearly fifty lines devoted to an appeal from France to Charles II to rule as an absolute king. At the end of it come the lines

> When she had spoke, a confus'd murmur rose
> Of French, Scots, Irish (all my[17] mortall foes).

The writer seems to have had in mind the general alarm at French ascendancy in the royal councils, and at the enrollment of Roman Catholics in the army on Blackheath for possible service against the Dutch. There are many references to "Irish Popish Officers" commissioned and Protestants dismissed, and to the two French generals, Schomberg and Feversham, in Grey's *Debates* in 1673 and early in 1674.

"Resigns his Crown to Angell Carwells trust . . .".

Louise de Quéroualle (Anglicized to Carwell) had accompanied Charles's sister, Henrietta, Duchess of Orleans, to Dover in the spring of 1670 when he, in return for a French pension and the offer of a French army, promised to declare his conversion to Roman Catholicism and to wage war on the Dutch when Louis

[16]*Ibid.*, II, 404.
[17]Britannia's.

XIV should be ready to assail them by land. Madame died a month later, and Charles was so grieved at his sister's death that the secret Treaty of Dover seemed in danger. Louis, aware of the impression she had made upon Charles at Dover, sent Louise de Quéroualle to England, where she promptly became a maid of honor to the Queen. Soon after the mock marriage in October, 1671, she became recognized as the favorite royal mistress and the incarnation of French influence. She was created Duchess of Portsmouth on August 19, 1673. In May, 1674, she was joined by her sister Henriette, who married the Earl of Pembroke towards the end of the year.[18] At this point line 169 may be interpolated for discussion— "Teach 'em to scorn the Carwells, Pembrookes, Nells." If it is certain that Pembroke is mentioned here as Henriette's husband, Mr. Margoliouth's argument that the poem was written after the marriage is unassailable. But, from the context, Pembroke, a debauched young man, seems to have been introduced as a type the youth of the nation should avoid.

"False Finch, Knave Anglesey misguide the seals."

This line is of present importance only as providing a date before which it could not have been composed—November 9, 1673, when Heneage Finch was named Lord Keeper.

Frequent adresses to my Charles I send

. . . .

Present to his thought his long scorn'd Parliament . . .

The second line may be interpreted as a reference to one of the two long prorogations already noticed. If this is the meaning, the writer is strangely inconsistent, for Parliament could not present addresses when prorogued. More to the point would be to find a time when Charles showed his contempt for Parliament by ignoring its wishes. Unfortunately, there are two such periods—in 1673-74, and in 1675. On October 20, 1673, the very day Parliament met, and before the King's speech had been delivered, the Commons drew up an address that the marriage of James, Duke of York, and Mary,

[18]G.E.C., *Complete Peerage* (London), VI (1895), 242, gives the date as May 20, 1675. But Marvell mentions the marriage in a letter dated November 6, 1674, and in another, December 19, he states that it had taken place on "Thursday" which would be December 17.

Duchess of Modena, be not consummated. When, ten days later, the King replied that the marriage had been completed according to the forms customary among princes, the Commons, the next day, again protested, alleging that the marriage would fill subjects with "endless jealousies and discontents" and would lead to alliances abroad "highly prejudicial, if not destructive, to the Interest of the very Protestant Religion itself." Thereupon Parliament was prorogued until January 7, 1674. Within the first week the Commons addressed the King to order the militia throughout the country to be ready, at an hour's warning, to suppress tumultuous meetings of Papists, but the royal reply was couched in general and vague terms. On January 13, Charles was asked to exclude first Lauderdale and then Buckingham from his presence and councils. No response being forthcoming, the House resolved to attend the King, who coolly answered that he would consider the advice about the two noblemen—a polite refusal. In the session from April to June, 1675, a further string of addresses against Lauderdale and a fresh series asking that English subjects in French military service be recalled were equally unavailing.

Up to this point the writer has followed the steps he took to discover whither the various clues led him. His peregrinations have occupied five years, from 1673 to 1678. But the time has now come to see whether or not the various signposts he has found do indicate a fixed date. The conclusion here reached is that "Britannia and Rawleigh" was composed early in 1674. The *terminus a quo* is provided by the reference to Finch. The *terminus ad quem* is settled by events in the House of Commons early in 1674. A careful examination of all the points raised shows that while some might be assigned to other times, there is no one time that will fit them all except early in 1674. Once the reader's sight is adjusted, all kinds of additional signs leap to the eye. The line, "And Commons' votes shall cut-nose guards disband," suggests the Commons' vote of February 7, 1674, that standing forces, other than the militia, were a great grievance and vexation. That the Irish are mentioned several times may be due to another address from the Lower House asking that the forces out of Ireland be no longer continued under arms in England. Charles replied on February 11 that he would reduce the army and·send the Irish back to Ireland. In both instances the satirist's lines would have had little point after the wishes of the Commons had been complied with.

One feature of the poem, perhaps the most interesting, has been left to the end. When Rawleigh urges Britannia to make one more effort to reclaim Charles II, she refuses, because the Stuart could not be divided from the tyrant. The question naturally arises, when would a well-informed political satirist be likely to determine that the King was incapable of reformation? The answer might well be, early in February, 1674.

An optimist might have imagined a year earlier that Charles was going to mend his ways. On March 8, 1673, he had bowed to the will of Parliament, canceled the obnoxious Declaration of Indulgence, and, on March 29, assented to the Test Act which required a denial of transubstantiation from all office holders. James, Duke of York, had resigned as Lord High Admiral, and one of the most profligate administrations England ever endured was gradually dissolved. By the end of the year hopes that Charles would pursue a Protestant policy abroad and rule constitutionally at home were seen to be fallacious. James continued to influence the royal councils, and to discredit Parliament, and a substantial French subsidy was received. Shaftesbury, regarded as "the one genuine Protestant in high office,"[19] was dismissed and brought his knowledge or suspicions of pro-Catholic intrigues to the aid of the opposition. The record already supplied above proved that the King had no intention of making Parliament "the bassis of his throne and Government." If optimism survived these shocks, it soared above evidence and common sense; it must have been inspired by either fanatical loyalty or an itching palm. Moreover, if it did survive them, it should have grown stronger and not died in 1675, when Danby, a Protestant and a supporter of William of Orange, the Protestant champion in Europe, was recognized as Chief Minister. Thus, by another route, we reach the same conclusion—that "Britannia and Rawleigh" was composed early in 1674.

GODFREY DAVIES

[19]David Ogg, *England in the Reign of Charles II* (Oxford: Clarendon Press, 1934), I, 380.

Friends of the Huntington Library

Notes and News

Newes from the New-World comes to the Friends as their memberships are renewed in 1946. It is the sixth annual souvenir printed by the Friends organization for distribution to its members, a pleasing little blue volume corresponding in format to others of a series, *The California Almanac for 1849, Bill of Rights,* and *A Letter from a Gold Miner.* Its editor, Louis B. Wright of the Library's research staff, explains on the title page that within "may be seene the excellent qualities of the Beastes of the Fielde, the Fish, and Fowl, As well as the singular and rare Vertues of the Earth and Air of that Goodly Land." More specifically, it contains excerpts from early publications and the text of two manuscripts in the Huntington Library collections: a manuscript letter written from Jamestown in Virginia, in November 1608, by Captain Peter Wynne to his patron, Sir John Egerton, later first Earl of Bridgewater; a tract, "Good Newes From Virginia," written by the Reverend Alexander Whitaker and published in London in 1613 by order of the Virginia Company; a manuscript letter of 1624 from Captain John Smith to the Society of Cordwainers of London (also reproduced in facsimile); an excerpt from the Reverend Francis Higginson's "New-Englands Plantation," published in London in 1630, dealing with "the Aire of New-England, with the Temper and Creatures in it;" and the facsimile of a stock certificate of the Virginia Company, dated April 4, 1610.

Members of the Friends formed a large proportion of the guests who attended the annual celebration of Founder's Day, held on Monday, February 25. In the main exhibition hall they heard the talk, "Obligations of Science," given by Dr. Edwin P. Hubble, member of the Board of Trustees of the Library, who has recently returned to Pasadena from four years as Chief Ballistician at the Research and Development Center of the Ordnance Department of the United States Army at Aberdeen Proving Ground, in Maryland. Before and after the talk, with other guests and members of the staff, they viewed the new exhibitions prepared for the occasion: One Hundred Photographs of California by Edward Weston; Early Mezzotints, Papers of Judge John W. North, and other Recent Gifts to the Library; Armorial Bindings; and the Works of Kate Greenaway.

List of Contributors

ROBERT G. CLELAND
Research Staff, Huntington Library

HAYDÉE NOYA
Manuscripts Department Staff, Huntington Library

HALLETT SMITH
Professor of English, Williams College

HELENE MAXWELL HOOKER
Assistant Editor, *Hollywood Quarterly*

GODFREY DAVIES
Research Staff, Huntington Library

To Contributors

Articles and notes contributed to *The Huntington Library Quarterly* should be typewritten on standard-size paper, double-spaced, with generous margins. Prose quotations which exceed six lines in length should be single-spaced, without quotation marks and without indentation, unless the quotation begins a paragraph. Verse quotations of more than two lines in length should be single-spaced and centered. Footnotes should be numbered consecutively throughout the article and indicated in the text by superior figures. They should appear at the bottom of the page (or, if the writer prefers, all together at the end of the article), single-spaced, the first line indented, preceded by the superior figure.

In matters of form the *Quarterly* follows the University of Chicago *Manual of Style* (10th ed.; 1937) and in spelling it follows the preferred use in *Webster's Dictionary* (2d ed., unabridged; 1937).

In quoted matter, unless there is strong reason for retaining the type peculiarities of the original, it is desirable to expand contractions, lower superior letters, substitute "v" for "u" (or vice versa), "j" for "i," "w" for "vv," etc., in accordance with modern usage. Greek should be transliterated, and long quotations in Latin, Greek, or other foreign languages should be translated. If desirable, the original language may be reproduced in footnotes. In every case clarity, both in typography and language, is the aim.

The ordinary citation of a book includes the author's name, the title of the book, place and date of publication, volume and page numbers. The title is underscored to indicate italics. [Example: V. S. Clark, *History of Manufactures in the United States* (New York, 1929), I, 38-43.] The title of an article in a periodical or continuing series should be inclosed in quotation marks and followed by the title of the periodical. [Example: Isaac Lippincott, "Industrial Influence of Lead in Missouri," *Journal of Political Economy*, XX (1931), 695-715.] If the work is an edited one, the title should be followed by the editor's name. [Example: *Speeches, Correspondence and Political Papers of Carl Schurz*, ed. Frederic Bancroft (New York, 1913), I, 55-57.] For a work lacking pagination, use the signature instead of page references: Sig. A3^v. If a work cited is in a series, the name of the series, inclosed in quotation marks, followed by the serial number, if given, should precede the place of publication. [Example: C. R. Fish, *The Civil Service and the Patronage* ("Harvard Historical Studies," XI; New York, 1905), pp. 102-3.] If a particular edition of a work is cited, the number of the edition precedes the place of publication. [Example: *A Manual of Style* (8th ed.; Chicago, 1925).]